Korean-American Youth Identity and 9/11
An Examination of Korean-American Ethnic Identity in Post - 9/11 America

Rev. Ham Suk-Hyun Studies in Asian Christianity
NUMBER 3
Heerak Christian Kim
Series Editor

Korean-American Youth Identity and 9/11
AN EXAMINATION OF KOREAN-AMERICAN ETHNIC IDENTITY IN POST - 9/11 AMERICA

Heerak Christian Kim

The Hermit Kingdom Press
Highland Park * Seoul * Bangalore * Cebu

Korean-American Youth Identity and 9/11: An Examination of Korean-American Ethnic Identity in Post-9/11 America
(Rev. Ham Suk-Hyun Studies in Asian Christianity, 3)

Copyright ©2008 Heerak Christian Kim

All rights reserved. No part of this book may be reproduced in any form or by any means, electronic or mechanical, including photocopying, recording, or by any information storage and retrieval system (including computer files in any form), without permission in writing from the publisher.

Hardcover ISBN13: 978-1-59689-077-0
Paperback ISBN13: 978-1-59689-078-7

Write To Address:
The Hermit Kingdom Press
P. O. Box 1226
Highland Park, NJ 08904-1226
The United States of America

Library of Congress Cataloging-in-Publication Data

Kim, H. C. (Heerak Christian)
  Korean-American youth identity and 9/11 : an examination of Korean-American ethnic identity in post-9/11 America / Heerak Christian Kim.
    p. cm. -- (Rev. Ham Suk-Hyun studies in Asian Christianity ; 3)
  Includes bibliographical references and index.
  ISBN 978-1-59689-077-0 (hardcover : alk. paper) -- ISBN 978-1-59689-078-7 (pbk. : alk. paper)
  1. Korean American youth--Social conditions. 2. Korean American youth--Religion. 3. Korean American youth--Ethnic identity. 4. September 11 Terrorist Attacks, 2001--Influence. I. Title.
  E184.K6K45 2008
  305.8957073--dc22
                                    2008019083

Dedicated to Professor Hilary Conroy of the University of Pennsylvania,
Who was my Undergraduate History Advisor
Who inspired me to be a historian of the highest rank

Table of Contents

Acknowledgments   iii

Chapter 1   1
"9/11 and Korean-American Youth: A Study on Two Opposing Forces Resulting from 9/11 on Korean-American Christianity"

Chapter 2   26
"Korean-American Youth in the General American Social Context"

Chapter 3   48
"The Nature of Korean-American Christianity"

Chapter 4   70
"Understanding the Korean-American Family"

Chapter 5   93
"Korean-American Youths, the American Work Place, and US Politics"

Chapter 6   111
"The Korean-American Conflict with African-Americans"

Chapter 7   124
"The Korean-American Youth Search for Group Identity"

Contents

Chapter 8   **156**
    "Korean-American Youth Dating and Marriage"

Conclusion   **185**

Bibliography   **197**

Index   **207**

Acknowledgement

I have interacted with many scholars on Korean studies and ethnic studies around the world, and I would like to personally thank the following scholars. Professor Jai Keun Choi of Yonsei University in South Korea has been an inspiration to me. I always learn from our conversations, and his research on modern Korean history spurs my thinking on Korean-American history. I would also like to thank Professor Sebastian Kim of York St. John University in England who is a leading scholar on ethnic studies as pertaining to India and Indians. Professor Kim was the Director of Christianity in Asia Project (CAP) at Cambridge University for two years, and we had the pleasure of collaborating in many important projects during his stay at Cambridge University. I appreciate his insights and kind encouragements. I would also like to thank Professor Grace Koh of School of Oriental and African Studies (SOAS) in London, who is an expert of ancient Korean history and literature. Paris- and Oxford-trained, Professor Koh's erudition regarding the cause and effect of Korean history and literature is helpful in understanding the residue impact on Korean identity among all Koreans around the world. Professor Gabriel Jonsson, the resident Korean expert of Sweden, who teaches at Stockholm University and serves as a consultant for the Swedish government and the European Union, has been a good friend over many years. He has read my book of poems relating to Korea, entitled *The Korean Soul*, and offered many praises, which made me blush with embarrassment but which also encouraged me to write more poetry on Korea. I would also like to thank Mr. Yi Munyol, a famous Korean writer of novels and short stories, for his encouragement to

Acknowledgment

pursue my literary interests relating to Korean poetry and literature. Professor Ra Jong-Il, the former Ambassador of the Republic of Korea to the United Kingdom, who is now the leading South Korean governmental expert on North Korea – South Korea relations, has also been very encouraging. As a scholar of Korean studies in his own right, he spurred my examination of how politics relating to North Korea impacts Koreans around the world in terms of identity. I thank Ambassador Ra for this new direction in research. I would also like to thank Professor Seungja Choi, who teaches the Korean language at Yale University. Her encouragement has meant a lot to me, and I still remember her words of encouragement 20 years ago to me to contribute to Korean studies. I would also like to thank my aunt, Soo Kyung Jun, who is currently the President of the Koreans Schools Association of the United States of America, whose membership boasts thousands of local Korean schools in the USA offering language, literature, and history instruction relating to all things Korean to Korean-American youths. Last but not least, I would like to thank Professor Hilary Conroy, who was my undergraduate history major advisor at the University of Pennsylvania. He has established himself as a world-famous expert of Korean and Japanese history as a scholar and has been very active as a policy maker/advisor on behalf of the US government since the days after World War 2 when he was stationed in Japan as an American dignitary and up to the present as he has frequently served as a consultant for the US government on policy issues relating to South Korea, North Korea, and Japan. Professor Conroy had confidence in me and encouraged me to pursue Korean history and distinguish myself as an expert of Korean history. This monograph represents in part a partial fulfilment of Professor Conroy's hope and dream for his "favorite" student. Thus, it is to my first advisor of history, Professor Hilary Conroy, that I dedicate this book in gratitude for his academic tutelage and encouragement.

Chapter 1:
"9/11 and Korean-American Youth: A Study on Two Opposing Forces Resulting from 9/11 on Korean-American Christianity"

The Korean American community has been deeply impacted by 9/11 and its aftermath. For many Koreans, it brought to fore questions about communal safety in the American context because the previously held assumption as to the safety of America was broken and the concept of North Korea as an axis-of-evil power became more relevant and "real." Many began to question how this would implicate South Korean immigrants in the United States. The question regarding the safety of Koreans in America as an immigrant community came to be externalized in two completely opposing tendencies. One trend was an aggressively conservatizing trend among the church-goers, pushing even historically left-leaning Korean churches closer toward the evangelical/fundamentalist direction. The other trend went the opposite direction with many individual Korean Christians leaving the church and abandoning institutional Christianity altogether, thereby leaving many Korean local congregations empty. This post-9/11 trend is most noticeable among those in the late teens and in college. In this chapter, I will describe the sociological phenomena of the two opposite forces that have impacted Korean-American Christianity after 9/11, particularly focusing on late-teen and college-age Koreans.

The starting point of any discussion on Korean-Americans must be on their perception of themselves or their understanding of their group identity. It is difficult to generalize about Korean-

American identity because there is a wide spectrum of who belong to this group. On the one hand, you have the FOB's, which stands for "Fresh Off the Boat." They are Korean immigrants who recently came from Korea and retain all traits that are distinctively Korean in nature. They generally speak in Korean. They subscribe to Korean fashion in clothing. Their mannerisms and way of behaving is "Korean" and not what would normally be described as "American" or "Western." On the other far end of the spectrum are those Koreans refer to as "Bananas." Bananas are Korean-Americans who have lived in America for a long-time and consciously work toward integrating into American way of life. Put in another way, Bananas are those who consciously work toward divesting themselves of what they perceive as Korean culture or Korean ways. Not all Bananas are American-born. In fact, some Bananas are quite recent immigrants; some may even have immigrated to the United States 3 or 4 years ago, or even less. Whereas FOBs are identified by their perpetual use of the Korean language and resorting to visible Korean customs and dress, Bananas are identified primarily by the company that they keep. Since "Banana" in colloquial discourse stands for those who are "yellow on the outside but white on the inside," it would not be surprising to see the label of Banana applied to Koreans who have mostly white friends. A clear visible evidence of a person's Banana status continues to be having a white spouse or significant other, like a white girlfriend. Of course in both cases – that of the FOB and the Banana – identity markers are more complex than the mere superficial descriptions. But certainly, on a popular Korean-American discourse level, these are the most simplistic ways to identify FOBs and Bananas – by the language they speak, the clothing they wear, and the friends they keep.

Most of the Korean-Americans do not neatly fall into the group of the FOBs and the Bananas. The majority of the Korean-Americans fall somewhere in-between. Of course, depending on which end of the spectrum a Korean-American is, she will identify other Koreans as FOBs and Bananas slightly differently. However, the general rule still applies. A Korean-American who speaks mostly in Korean and have mostly Korean-American friends tend to be FOBs and Korean-Americans who have predominantly white friends and speak only in English are Bananas. The fact that most Korean-Americans fall between these two antipodal ends is recognized by most Koreans, although they may not verbalize it in such terms explicitly or publicly. In a sense, we can describe this understanding as culturally innate or a subliminal part of the Korean-American consciousness. The reality is assumed to be fact, and this reality is rarely questioned.

The fact of Korean-American assumption regarding the linear spectrum between the FOB and the Banana is visible in the way Korean-Americans describe themselves. Korean-Americans have developed a decimal point system to describe themselves. For instance, a Korean who is just from Korea is 1st generation Korean-American. Korean who came from Korea at the age of about 13 years old is a 1.5 generation Korean-American.[1] And a Korean who came from Korea at the age of 7 years old is a 1.75 Korean-American. A Korean who immigrated from Korea at the age of 17 is a 1.2 Korean. Although the decimal point has not been systematized per se, there is a popular understanding of what a 1.5 is and 1.75 is and 1.2 is. The guideline is set by unspoken communal consent that assumes the spectrum between the FOB and Banana.

What is a 2nd generation Korean-American? 2nd generation Korean-American in the Korean-American cultural context is a

---

[1] Won Moo Hurh defines the 1.5 generation Korean-American in this way: "At this point of discussion, however, the 1.5 generation can ideally-typically be defined as bilingual and bicultural Korean-American who immigrated to the United States in early or middle adolescence (generally between the ages of 11 and 16). Simply put, the adolescent immigration, bilingualism, and biculturalism constitute a unique sociocultural and existential context of Korean-American whose life course appears to be quite different from that of the first and second generation immigrants" (Won Moo Hurh, "The 1.5 Generation: A Cornerstone of the Korean-American Ethnic Community," *The Emerging Generation of Korean-Americans*, eds. Ho-Youn Kwon and Shin Kim [Seoul: Kyung Hee University Press, 1993, pp. 47-79], p. 50).

Korean who is born in the USA to parents who immigrated to the USA. Interestingly enough, children born to 1st generation Korean-Americans and children born to 1.5 Korean-Americans are both said to be 2nd generation Koreans. The reason that the distinction is not made between the two can be attributed to the relative newness of the majority of Korean-Americans in the USA. Most households have parents who are 1st generation. Rarely will one find 3rd generation Korean-Americans – Korean-Americans who are born in America to parents who are born in America. The Korean-American immigration experience is about a generation (calculated at 35 years) or less.² The 1970 census found about 70,000 Koreans residing in the USA. But the number increased rapidly since then by 30,000 Koreans every year. In 1976, about 290,000 Koreans were resident in the United States. And the 1980 US census numbered Koreans at 354,529.³ Furthermore, a demographic study of Los Angeles in 1979 revealed that almost 81% of Koreans living in the Los Angeles area had been living in LA for 7 years or less. About two-thirds had lived in the United States for seven years or less. And the mean was 6.5 years.⁴ Tae-Hwan Kwak and Seong Hyong Lee note that in 1990, the Korean-American population was estimated to be 1.3 million. The majority of them immigrated to the USA since 1965 when the US government lifted the ban on immigration from Asia. Kwak and Lee state in the introduction to their edited book, *The Korean-American Community: Present and Future*, that most of the 1.3 million Koreans in 1990

---

² The greatest wave of Korean immigration started in the late 1960s and in the 1970s because of two factors: (1) Korean President Park Chung-Hee's positive emigration policy and (2) the 1965 revision of United States immigration laws (P.L. 89-236) (Ji-Yeon Yuh, *Beyond the Shadow of Camptown: Korean Military Brides in America* [New York: New York University Press, 2002], p. 66).
³ Won Moo Hurh and Kwang Chung Kim, *Korean Immigrants in America: A Structural Analysis of Ethnic Confinement and Adhesive Adaptation* (Rutherford: Associated University Presses, 1984), p. 21.
⁴ Hurh and Kim, *Korean Immigrants in America*, p. 57.

represent the wave of immigration in 1970s and 1980s.[5] And Won Moo Hurh in his 1998 book states: "More than two-thirds of the current Korean population in the United States are foreign-born, and the majority of them arrived after 1970."[6] It is clear how recent Korean immigration in the United States is. The majority of Korean-Americans living in the USA were born in Korea or had parents born in Korea. This is the current reality. Because of the relative newness of Korean immigration, the language is limited in terms of the decimal point system applied between the 2nd generation and the 3rd generation. One will find many Korean-Americans who are 1.5 or 1.7 or 1.2,[7] but one will never find Koreans who are 2.5. This is not a part of the Korean-American discourse on popular or academic levels. There is only the 2nd generation and the 3rd generation; there is no decimal point between these two spectrums.

Korean-Americans have developed this system instinctively without any academic dictating of the point system. No one knows who started the discourse. It just became completely adopted by Korean-Americans all over the USA. It can be seen as an integral part of Korean-American culture. It became normative spontaneously. Won Moo Hurh writes regarding the term "the 1.5 generation": "The term was coined in the Korean community around 1980. Although the Japanese terms for first-, second-, and third-generation immigrants – *issei*, *nisei*, and *sansei* – are found in *Webster's Dictionary*, a term such as '1.5 generation' has not been used with reference to other immigrant groups."[8] I would argue that the reason for this is because of the spectrum between the FOB

---

[5] Tae-Hwan Kwak and Seong Hyong Lee, *The Korean-American Community: Present and Future* (Seoul: Kyungnam University Press, 1991), p. 1.
[6] Won Moo Hurh, *The Korean Americans* (Westport: Greenwood Press, 1998), p. xv.
[7] June Ha, "1.5 and 2.0 Generation of Korean Women," *The Emerging Generation of Korean-Americans*, eds. Ho-Youn Kwon and Shin Kim (Seoul: Kyung Hee University Press, 1993, pp. 225-235), p. 229.
[8] Hurh, *The Korean Americans*, p. 164.

and the Banana that operates distinctively in the Korean-American context. In a way, the reality of the FOB and the Banana explains the innate tensions within the Korean-American community, wavering between the Mother Country that they left behind and the New Land where they now live.

The Korean-American decimal point system is innately Korean-American. Most ethnographers do not even know of the point system. Generally, anthropologists and sociologists refer to first American born immigrants as 1st generation Americans, with whichever ethnic title attached to them. Thus, if a couple immigrated from Ireland, their baby born in America would be first generation Irish-American. The parents would be immigrants and would not really have a generation attached to them. This assumption is based on the fact that sociologists and anthropologists attribute the identity of the parents to the country they immigrated from. So, the Irish immigrant couple are Irish and not really Irish-Americans, per se. They are Irish immigrants in America. Even American laws seem to support this presupposition. As powerful as Governor Arnold Schwartzeneggar is, he is treated by a different set of laws from his children who are born in the USA. Governor Schwarzeneggar is not American per se by the standards of anthropologists and sociologists. He is an Austrian immigrant in America who has been naturalized and became an American citizen. Thus, if Governor Schwarzeneggar breaks a law, he can be extradited to Austria. He is not really American the way his children are. They cannot be extradited to Austria because they are not seen as Austrian in any legal sense of the term or sociological sense of the term. They are first generation Americans. In contrast, Governor Schwarzeneggar is not really American and that is why he cannot become a US President by law. Not only can he be extradited to Austria, the American law fundamentally assumes that he is not fully loyal to the USA by the virtue of his immigration.

American custom, academia, and laws perceive first generation Americans as those who are born in America to immigrants from another country. Only the Korean-Americans in the USA view things differently and utilize their own system of attaching generation-system within the community. What are we to make of this? I would argue that this reality points to the way Korean-Americans view themselves in the American context. First of all, they rebel – whether they are aware of it or not – against the cultural, academic, and legal mores of America in the way they perceive themselves. This can be approached from various angles. I would like to emphasize that the reason for this approach is that they were concerned more with the spectrum between the FOB and the Banana.

Why have Koreans been so concerned about this spectrum? It goes to the history of the Korean people. Korea is called the Hermit Kingdom for a reason. It has remained radically isolationist. Although China called white people, "white devils," they gave white people access to China relatively early. This was the case with Japan as well. Despite the highly anti-western and anti-white sentiment floating around in Japan, Japan welcomed white individuals into Japan relatively early in its modern history. In contrast, Koreans intentionally held off welcoming westerners in. Korea was the last nation in East Asia to establish normalized relations with the United States. This was done in 1882 through the signing of the Korean-American Treaty in 1882.[9] The fear of the Banana factor is a part of the conscious fear of the westerner in the Korean community.

Every Korean-American will tell you that their parents wanted one thing from them – that was that they marry a Korean.[10] Most Korean-American parents have historically threatened to dis-

---

[9] Hurh and Kim, *Korean Immigrants in America*, p. 39. The Korean-American Treaty of 1882 is also known as "The Chemulpo Treaty" or "The Treaty of Amity and Commerce."

[10] Sunok Chon Pai, "The Changing Role of Korean-Americans," *The Emerging Generation of Korean-Americans*, eds. Ho-Youn Kwon and Shin Kim (Seoul: Kyung Hee University Press, 1993, pp. 215-224), pp. 218-219.

own their children if they married white.[11] This cultural standard is operating still in many Korean families. Chon S. Edwards, a Korean who married a white American, states that even reputable Koreans with high social status living in the United States would be ashamed if their children married white. Often, the wedding will be done "in secret" and their close Korean friends not invited to the wedding.[12] Perhaps, Ji-Yeon Yuh's comments about Korean women who married white American soldiers best explain the situation. Yuh writes regarding these Korean women of intermarriage: "For second-generation Korean Americans, they were the women sitting alone, without husbands, during church service and fellowship, the ones they'd ignored because everyone else did."[13] It is this anti-white sentiment that developed the Banana system, or the 1.5 system of identification. The sentiment of the Korean immigrant parents have been internalized in their children. It is not surprising, therefore, that even 2nd generation Koreans in California refuse to marry non-Koreans and often ostracize Koreans in their midst who marry non-Koreans. The Banana fear is an integral part of the Korean-American experience that is connected to the Korean historical experience.

A part of the reason for the phenomena is due to what Won Moo Hurh and Kwang Chung Kim call "adhesive adaptation" of Korean-Americans to the American context.[14] What that means is that Korean-Americans tend to keep the Korean core – such as Korean traditional culture and Korean social-networks – while being

---

[11] It would not be wrong to describe anti-white sentiment as historical for Korean-Americans. Of the Korean males in the United States during 1912-1924, those who could not find Koreans remained single until their death – some 3000 males. Only 104 Korean males married non-Koreans during this period, and they married Asian-looking women (Romanzo Adams, *Interracial Marriage in Hawaii* [Montclair: Patterson Smith, 1937], p. 336-337).
[12] Chon S. Edwards, *I Am Also A Daughter of Korea* (Seoul: Mi-Rae-Mun-Wha-Sa, 1988), p. 111 [in Korean].
[13] Yuh, *Beyond the Shadow of Camptown: Korean Military Brides in America*, p. 3.
[14] Hurh and Kim, *Korean Immigrant in America*, p. 27.

Americanized culturally and socially. "Americanization" is on the surface level and for public consumption in the larger American context. However, on a fundamental level Korean-Americans tend to value their Korean identity and culture. What is quite relevant in this regard is the conscious sentiment in the Korean-American community that Korean-Americans should be closely tied to things Korean regardless of how long they have been in the United States. Sang-O Rhee expresses this sentiment: "What we desire most is that the second generation should identify with the Korean society in America and Korea and develop positive attitudes towards them. If this can be successfully accomplished through the Korean education system, we can develop responsible citizens of a pluralistic society of multi-language and culture. This type of adaptation is called 'harmonious self-identity of love America and love Korea.'"[15] Sang-O Rhee is voicing a normative desire in the Korean-American community, seeking preservation of Korean culture among Korean-Americans born in the USA. This is quite visible in the Korean-American church context. It is not surprising, therefore, to find Korean-American churches that have thousands of members in Los Angeles, Anaheim, Baltimore, New York, etc. which only speak Korean and preserve Korean ways. No other ethnic group in the USA has had such a phenomenon. Many German-Americans are Christians. But there are no churches with thousands of German-Americans. The same goes for Chinese-Americans. There are many Chinese-American Christians but it is hard to find a Chinese church in any city that numbers over a thousand.

The Korean-American church functions as a cultural center of the Korean-American people as well as its religious center. This was the case from the beginning of Korean immigration, which

---

[15] Sang-O Rhee, "The Leaders of 21st Century Korean Communities in America: The Role of Second Generation Education," *The Korean-American Community: Present and Future*, eds. Tae-Hwan Kwak and Seong Hyong Lee (Seoul: Kyungnam University Press, 1991, pp. 157-179), p. 172.

was in 1903 in Hawaii.[16] Early Korean settlers made Christian worship their first major social event after immigrating to the USA. For instance, early Koreans (some 300 Christians and 30 preachers who followed the immigrants everywhere) set up a Christian church on July 5, 1903, in Mokolia, Oahu, and another Christian church on River Street, Honolulu, on November 10, 1903.[17] This trend of setting up Korean churches as a Korean cultural center along with a place of religious worship for Koreans still characterizes the Korean-American community. Hurh and Kim write: "The Korean immigrants appear, therefore, to crave both types of fellowship – spiritual (Christian) fellowship *and* ethnic fellowship…. The Korean ethnic church provides best both fellowships for the immigrant…."[18] Thus, it would not be surprising that if any Korean-American clergy adopts a Banana stance, he will lose his church membership like dust in the wind.[19] For instance, if a Korean-American church of 3,000 members hires a senior pastor who prefers Banana ways and encourages marrying white people, Korean-American members will leave that church and find a Korean-American church that is more dedicated to Korean ways.[20] The Korean-American church is a cultural center for the Korean-

---

[16] Hurh and Kim, *Korean Immigrants in America*, p. 47.
[17] Warren Y. Kim, *Koreans in America* (Seoul: Po Chin Chai Printing Co. Ltd., 1971), p. 28.
[18] Hurh and Kim, *Korean Immigrants in America*, p. 134.
[19] A study of Korean-American Christians in Chicago revealed that 97%, regardless of Christian denomination, preferred an ethnically Korean church. Only 3% attended an American church that was not specifically ethnic Korean (Hurh, *The Korean Americans*, p. 107).
[20] A 1979 survey shows that Koreans value their Korean identity. 94.7% of males and 94.4 % of the females were proud to be born ethnically Korean. Furthermore, 90.4% of the males and 89.2% of the females state that the Korean language should be taught. Furthermore, over 60% were against intermarriage. And the majority of those who approved intermarriage approved it only on the basis of true love and understanding (Huhr and Kim, *Korean Immigrants in America*, p. 79).

American people and the central thrust of the Korean-American culture tends to be anti-Banana.[21]

Thus, even 3rd generation Korean-Americans are ashamed if they cannot speak Korean.[22] And those who speak even a few sentences boast and lie and say that they can speak good Korean.[23] In the Korean-American cultural matrix of the Korean-American

---

[21] In this regard, the statement of Hurh and Kim is significant: "In sharp contrast to the findings on acculturation, most of the dimensions of ethnic attachment are *not* related to the length of residence in the United States. ...regardless of the length of residence, a high proportion of our respondents subscribe to Korean newspapers, prefer to associate with Koreans, and prefer to attend the Korean ethnic church. Almost all of them also indicate their strong sense of family priority, ethnic pride, and preference for teaching Korean language to their children.... The educational statuses also have no bearing on the degree of ethnic attachment.... Generally, most of the respondents show strong feelings of ethnic attachment regardless of the levels of their education..." (Hurh and Kim, *Korean Immigrants in America*, p. 84). Anyone who visits a Korean church today can attest to the lasting impact of this reality as an integral Korean-American experience. Furthermore, a visit to UCLA and UC Berkeley will prove most of this to be true for the youngest generation of Korean-Americans, today.

[22] A part of the reason for the emphasis in speaking Korean relates to Korean history during the Japanese period where Koreans were forbidden to speak Korean. Regarding this period, Sunny Che writes: "As one of the first colonial acts, Japan took the five-year-old crown prince of Korea to Japan to be reared in the Japanese imperial household and eventually married to a Japanese princess. She banned the Korean language and national symbols – flag, flower, and anthem – and instituted Japanese laws and Japanese as the official language. The government bureaucracy, commerce, and schools were conducted all in Japanese" (Sunny Che, *Forever Alien: A Korean Memoir, 1930-1951* [Jefferson: McFarland and Company, Inc. 2000], p. 7).

[23] Speaking of Korean is very important to the Korean-American community. According to the 1970 Census, 91% of the foreign-born Koreans stated that Korean was their primary language. And in the 1973 Asian-American Field Study of Koreatown, Los Angeles, 98% of Korean-Americans said that they used Korean as their primary language (Eui-Young Yu, "Koreans in America: Social and Economic Adjustments," *The Korean Immigrant in America*, eds. Byong-Suh Kim and Sang Hyun Lee [Montclair: The Association of Christian Scholars in North America, Inc., 1980, pp. 75-98], p. 88).

church, the Banana factor is feared, shunned, and hated. It is not surprising, therefore, to see that many Korean-Americans actually see teaching of the Korean language and culture as an integral mission of the Korean-American church. Yong Choon Kim writes: "The education of the second generation of Koreans is one of the most important tasks of the Korean church for the healthy progress of the Korean-American community. For this task Korean churches in America should make a special effort to continue teaching the Korean language along with Christian education."[24] One of the reasons why Korean-American churches have been so successful in America in contrast to other Asian ethnic churches is simply due to the fact that Korean-American churches have been aggressively pro-Korean and anti-white.[25]

The anti-white sentiment persisting in the Korean community has been enhanced in the Los Angeles Riots in 1992 when white American leaders (who controlled most of Los Angeles, including the police, government agencies, and the media) ignored pleas for help by Koreans. Koreans had given a lot of donations to police charities, election campaign funds, and other types of support for white leaders of Los Angeles.[26] Most Koreans felt be-

---

[24] Yong Choon Kim, "The Protestant Church and the Korean-American Community," *The Korean-American Community: Present and Future*, eds. Tae-Hwan Kwak and Seong Hyong Lee (Seoul: Kyungnam University Press, 1991, pp. 195-209), p. 198.

[25] This comment by Hurh and Kim is very important to understanding the experience of 2nd and 3rd generation Korean-Americans: "Simply put, the more closely Korean immigrants identify themselves with their WASP peers, the more they will experience heightened feelings of relative deprivation, social alienation, and identity ambivalence. At this point, the degree of the immigrant's life satisfaction (psychological adaptation) and their desire for assimilation (sociocultural adaptation) may start to decline. To mitigate the problematic situation, some immigrants may shift their reference group back to their own ethnic group (Koreans) or some may seek their identity and reference group elsewhere.... ...the relationship between the length of sojourn and the degree of adaptation (life satisfaction) may not be linear but rather quasicurvilinear..." (Hurh and Kim, *Korean Immigrants in America*, p. 140).

[26] Hurh, *The Korean Americans*, p. 121.

trayed, and pro-white factions in Korean communities were silenced for the foreseeable future. This fuelled greater anti-white sentiment in Korean-American churches. As a corollary, more Korean-American churches embraced things Korean, more aggressively. It would be difficult to find a Korean-American church that does not sing the Korean national anthem on Korean Independence Day (August 15th). In contrast, one will almost never find a Korean-American church singing the American national anthem, ever. One of the reasons why Korean Christianity combined with Korean nationalism is that those who attacked Koreans attacked Korean Christianity, historically. This was the case during the Japanese Occupation, when Korean nationalism became identified with Korean Christian martyrs. And this was the case during the Korean War when anti-Communism became identified with Korean Christianity. It was a fact that Korean Christians were sought out by Communists and killed for their Christian faith. For many Koreans, it became an integral part of their national identity as Koreans in the Japanese Occupation period and South Korean identity in the Korean War.

It does not really matter (on the popular level) how accurate the perception is (although it is quite accurate). The fact is that the communal memory hinges on this perceived reality. It may, in fact, not be *completely* the case in true Korean history. But this perception has been perpetuated within Korean Christianity and in Korean Christian pulpits. And thus, it is an integral part of the Korean collective memory and communal consciousness. If one does not understand this reality of the Korean Christian experience, which cannot be separated from Korean historical experiences for Korean-Americans, then she will not understand the Korean-American experience. Unfortunately, not much study has been done on this aspect of Korean-American identity. I hope to rectify this error in academia through a more indepth study in the future, particularly on this specific topic.

The extent to which this reality is fact for Korean-Americans is attested by the fact that almost 100 per cent of Korean-American college students will say that they have been to a Christian church in their youth.[27] Even parents who are non-Christians often sent their children to Korean churches for Korean cultural experiences. It is only a very recent phenomenon that some Koreans have started to rally around the Buddhist temple. This reality is evident when we look at the case of Chicago. In 1997, there were estimated 100,000 Koreans in the Chicago area. There were 196 Korean-American churches, primarily conducting their programs in the Korean language. In contrast, there were only 5 Buddhist temples.[28] Chicago actually has one of the largest Korean Buddhist communities, in terms of percentage, but still only about 4.2% of Korean-Americans in Chicago are Buddhist. In Los Angeles, only about 1.5% of the Korean-Americans are Buddhist.[29] For Korean-Americans, Buddhism was a non-factor for much of its immigration history.

    The beginning of Korean Buddhism in the United States is dated to 1964, when Soh Kyongbo, a Korean Buddhist monk, arrived in Philadelphia to pursue his Ph.D. studies at Temple University. Soh Kyongbo led a small Buddhist meditation group while he was a Ph.D. student at Temple University. But Korean Buddhism did not take a strong hold in Temple University or the city of Philadelphia, where the university is found. In fact, Korean Buddhism was marginalized within the Korean-American community as Korean-American churches thrived in American cities, including Philadelphia. In the early period of Korean Buddhism in America, many of the Buddhist movements were, in fact, scattered away from major Korean population centers, such as Los Angeles, Chicago, and New York. For instance, Kim Samu, a Korean Buddhist monk, set up Zen Lotus Societies in Toronto, Canada, and Ann Arbor, Michigan, in the 1970s. There were hardly any Kore-

---

[27] A recent survey shows 70% of all Los Angeles Koreans and 77% of all Chicago Koreans are active Christians (Hurh, *The Korean Americans*, p. 107).
[28] Hurh, *The Korean Americans*, p. 106.
[29] Hurh, *The Korean Americans*, p. 114.

ans in these cities at the time. Another Korean Buddhist leader, Sungsan, set up a Son Center in Providence, Rhode Island, in 1972.[30] There were hardly any Koreans there at the time. Eventually, Buddhist movements spread to population centers of Korean immigration, like Los Angeles and New York. But it is significant that Buddhism started in the fringes of the Korean-American community.[31] In this sense, Korean historical experience in America is vastly different from that of other immigrants from other Buddhist lands, such as China and Japan, which had a visible Buddhist population in the USA from the very beginning. Korean-Americans were completely different. Many Koreans abandoned Buddhism when they immigrated to the USA. They saw their immigration as immigrating to Christianity. Although many Korean-American parents may not have actively converted to Christianity, as immigrants to a new land who left Korea and Korean Buddhism behind they were willing to attend a Christian church and subscribe to the Christianity of America. The fact that Korean-American churches functioned as Korean-American cultural centers[32] made the transition easy and many Korean-Americans readily "converted" to Christianity in the context of the Korean-American immigrant life and the Korean-American church.

Present-day high school students and college students who are Korean-Americans must be understood in light of this historical experience of Korean-Americans. The majority of them have been to a Christian church in America and many of them have been

---

[30] Grant S. Lee, "The Future of Korean-American Buddhism," *The Korean-American Community: Present and Future*, eds. Tae-Hwan Kwak (Seoul: Kyungnam University Press, 1991, pp. 231-248), p. 233.

[31] In fact, Kim Samu and Sungsan worked primarily with white Americans and not Korean-Americans (Lee, "The Future of Korean-American Buddhism," p. 233).

[32] In contrast, Korean Buddhist centers were not Korean cultural centers in America. Almost all major Korean Buddhist centers not only targeted white Americans, Korean Buddhist monks trained white Americans to be their successors. In some Buddhist centers, 90% of the followers were white and 10% Asians (Lee, "The Future of Korean-American Buddhism," p. 245).

active participants. For many Korean-American youths, their Korean-American identity is closely tied to their experience in a Korean-American church. In this light, it is understandable why the Korean-American church experienced a great shock to the system with 9/11. 9/11 shocked Korean-Americans thoroughly and the shock manifested itself visibly in the setting of the Korean-American church.

What happened? In terms of the Korean-American experience, Korean-American immigrants were shocked in religious terms. Most Korean-Americans not only changed their country but their religion when they immigrated to the USA. Most Korean Buddhists abandoned Buddhism and many actively converted to Christianity. It is not surprising to find some churches with something like 80 per cent of its members being converts to Christianity. They converted after they came to the USA as immigrants. This seems to be in line with Korean immigration to the United States since the first immigration of 1903. Regarding the first wave of Korean-immigrants, Bong-Youn Choy writes that 40% were Christians but most Korean immigrants – including non-Christians eventually became Christian church-goers.[33] For many of these Korean-American immigrants, they identified America with a Christian land. They identified the blessings of America in the areas of economy and military in terms of its Christian identity. For Korean immigrants, the USA was a great country because it was Christian. They immigrated to America, the great nation, and they adopted Christianity, the great religion. The Korean-American church with its focus on Korean cultural identity made the transition in religious identity that much smoother. They could be Koreans and be Christians and live in the Christian land as Korean Christians. In fact, it would not be wrong to say that Koreans did not really see themselves as becoming naturalized as American citizens – rather, they perceived themselves as being Koreans in America who became Christians. For many of them, Christianity

---

[33] Bong-Youn Choy, *Koreans in America* (Chicago: Nelson Hall, 1979), p. 77.

was their identity that they shared with Americans. If one were to ask a Korean today what nationality he has, a typical Korean would say "Korean" even though he holds the US Passport and had to give up the Korean passport and Korean citizenship. One would be hard-pressed to find a Korean, even a 2nd generation Korean, who will refer to himself as an American.

Within the Korean-American experience, "American" identity meant being "Christian." This allowed Koreans to maintain their Korean heritage and continue the Hermit Kingdom ways while being fiercely loyal to the USA. This is a reason why Korean-Americans comprise the greatest percentage of Asian-Americans at West Point and other US military academies. Every Korean-American clergy will pray for America as a Christian nation that God should protect. Korean-Americans are patriotic to America not because they see value in their American citizenship but because their Korean-American identity became "Korean-American Christian"[34] identity and so they found solidarity with America the Christian nation on a religious level. There was never confusion among Korean-Americans regarding their loyalty to America the nation. Korean-Americans were loyal to and remain loyal to Korea as their "nation" despite their USA citizenship. They do not see a contradiction between being loyal to Korea "their nation" and being loyal to American "the Christian nation."[35] In fact, given the persecution that Korean Christianity suf-

---

[34] The fact that Korean-American identity became integrally intertwined with Christian identity is highlighted by *Korea Week* of February 1978. Only 12% of the total population in South Korea were affiliated with a Christian church. In contrast, 70% of Korean-Americans at the comparable time were affiliated with a Christian church in the USA (Hurh and Kim, *Korean Immigrants in America*, pp. 129-130). Many of the Korean-Americans who were affiliated with a Christian church were recent converts to Christianity after their immigration.

[35] This contrasts with the generic anti-American sentiment which has dominated South Korea for decades, especially as South Korea views the United States as its economic rival (Chongho Kim, "Temptation to Conform and Call to Transform," *The Emerging Generation of Korean-Americans*, eds. Ho-Youn Kwon and Shin Kim [Seoul: Kyung Hee University Press, 1993, pp. 253-263], p. 257).

fered in the last 100 years, if push comes to shove, they would be more loyal to the Christian nation over Korea. This was the case in the Korean War. Communists were killing Korean Christians, so Koreans in the South chose to die as Christians at the hands of their relatives from North Korea.

9/11 changed a lot of things. First of all, for many Korean-Americans, it proved that the Triune God of Heaven no longer protected America. How could the Christian God allow a small band of unsophisticated terrorists to highjack American planes right under the noses of American security and the most highly safeguarded place in American public life – the airport system – and to use American planes against American buildings? Surely, the Triune God of Heaven took away his protection from the country for such things to happen.

9/11 imbued Korean-Americans with doubt about America as a nation blessed by God. Since the identity of America as a Christian nation was firmly fixed in the Korean-American consciousness,[36] doubting America's divine protection encourage doubting the veracity of Christianity itself. Unlike white Christian evangelical Christians who started questioning the Christian identity of America since the 1920s and even chose to separate themselves from American politics in pursuit of Christian holiness and

---

[36] From the earliest period of Korean immigration to the United States, there was the perception that the USA is a Christian country. This perception became ingrained in the Korean-American consciousness. Hyung-Chan Kim criticizes this perception and even blames it as having had a negative impact on the Korean people. Kim writes: "It is tragic, particularly in view of the fact that so much of the energy and resources of the church were diverted to an unrealistic and naïve notion that the leaders and followers of 'Christian America,' when sufficiently supplicated by their fellow Korean Christians, would assist the Koreans in their fight against Imperial Japan" (Huyung-Chan Kim, "The History and Role of the Church in the Korean American Community," *The Korean Diaspora: Historical and Sociological Studies of Korean Immigration and Assimilation in North America*, ed. Hyung-Chan Kim [Santa Barbara: ABC-Clio, Inc., 1977, pp. 47-63], p. 60).

Christian identity (calling themselves "Fundamentalists"), Korean-American Christians identified America with Christianity.

Korean-American clergy encouraged this identity. Korean-Americans frequently pray for the USA and every time, they would pray that God protect the Christian nation of America. Korean-American pastors frequently preach about American missionaries bringing Christianity to Korea. When Korean-American clergy chastise Korea, they will not use any other nation on earth except for America to chastise Korea with, because America is a Christian nation, "founded by the Puritans." Thus, Korean-American church teachings along with individual Korean-American understanding of what America is – a Christian nation – encouraged the doubt that was created among Korean-Americans after 9/11. For many, it was conclusive evidence that Christianity was not true and that God of the Americans was false.

Of course, evangelical Christians who are white in America have been clamoring for decades that America is a secular nation with a secular agenda and not a Christian goal. But they are a part of the American society, experience, and discourse. Korean-Americans choose to be outside of that. Not everyone would say that Koreans had a choice in the matter. Sang Hyun Lee writes that by being non-white, Koreans in America are permanent outsiders even if they are more westernized than many of the white immigrants.[37] This applies to Korean-Americans born in the United States and their descendants, as well. Whether Korean-Americans are outside of the American mainstream by choice or not, the effect is the same. Korean-Americans view America through the lens of Korean-American identity and society. In other words, most Korean-Americans only know of America that the

---

[37] Sang Hyun Lee, "Called to be Pilgrims: Toward a Theology within the Korean Immigrant Context," *The Korean Immigrant in America*, eds. Byong-suh Kim and Sang Hyun Lee (Montclair: The Association of Korean Christian Scholars in North America, Inc., 1980, pp. 37-74), p. 40.

Korean-American church painted in rosy colors, through the lens of Korean Christianity.[38]

Thus, 9/11 encouraged a mass exodus of Korean-Americans from Christianity. Korean-American churches became empty as Korean-Americans left the Korean-American church as they chose to abandon Christianity, which 9/11 proved to be a false religion in their mind. Many of them in fact went back to their old religion of Buddhism.[39] And throughout Los Angeles and elsewhere, there was a revival of Buddhism among Koreans. This trend also manifested itself among the Korean-American young. Korean-American high school students and college students started to leave the Christian church in massive numbers. In some Korean-American churches, the college group became non-existent as high school students who went to college refused to go to church.

However, for the younger generation, the departure from Christian churches created a different reality than for their parents. Their parents were originally Buddhists, so they traded in their Christian identity card for a Buddhist one when they decided to

---

[38] Sang Hyun Lee describes the nature of Korean Christianity: "Under the influence of the westernized Christianity, Korean cultural past has been thought of as something that we must leave behind us. We were brought up perhaps with a greater familiarity with such names as Moses, Joseph, Noah, and Santa Claus than with such names as Won Hyo, Lee Toi Ge, and even Tan Gun. I remember the shocking experience I had a few years ago when I realized that I do not know enough Korean religious and philosophical personages even to count on my fingers! Now here in America, our four thousand year old history is almost totally invisible" (Sang Hyun Lee, "Called to be Pilgrims," p. 53). Lee's comments highlight the pro-Christian and pro-American (by extension) influence on Korean Christianity which is even willing to abandon some of its cultural past and historical heritage in support of Christianity or what is perceived as a Christian culture by Korean Christians.

[39] Although the Yi Dynasty of the Choson period (1392-1910) pushed Confucianism and persecuted Buddhists, Buddhism actually grew among the people more so than it did in times of peace. Even now, Buddhism claims the largest number of the Korean population (Yong-Joon Choi, *Dialogue and Antithesis: A Philosophical Study on the Significance of herman Dooyeweerd's Transcendental Critique* [Cheltenham: The Hermit Kingdom Press, 2006], pp. 276-278).

leave their Christian churches. Thus, they participated in the revival of Korean Buddhism in America. Unlike their parents, Korean teenagers and college students, many of them having been born in the USA, had no experience with Buddhism. They did not know what it was. They have never practiced a single Buddhist ritual in their life. Thus, when they left Christianity, they did not see Buddhism as an alternative. For many Korean-American teenagers and college students, they did not know what the alternative to Christianity was. Many of them blended into general secular culture without knowing what it was or what it meant for them. What 9/11 did for many Korean teenagers and college students was to push them away from Christianity without any clear direction. So, they left Christianity. Most of them did not adopt another religion. Since 9/11 is relatively new, we can describe the point where they currently are as a state of flight. They just wanted to abandon Christianity.

It was not too difficult for Korean-American youth to abandon Christianity, which they saw as a part of the oppressive white culture. The majority of Asian-Americans believe that they are marginalized in the USA. And Asian-American youth in the USA do not fit in with cultural institutions tied to the Old Country, either. Thus, it is not difficult to see how an event like 9/11 can easily unglue Korean-American teens from Korean-American churches and the Christianity they were taught in these churches. Since 9/11, many Korean-American youths have been drifting away from the Korean-American church without any clear direction. Interestingly enough, many Korean-American churches are abandoning the pro-American position they have held before 9/11. Since 9/11 was relatively recent, it is hard to access completely the nature of the Korean-American exodus from Korean-American churches and the new direction of Korean-American churches. Some churches are reporting over 90% of their youth leaving their church, currently.

What this has done is to create a very de-stabilizing reality for the Korean-American community. The mass exodus away from Christianity without any clear direction has created a communal vacuum. The Korean-American church still is the only real Korean cultural center. Sang Hyun Lee emphasizes the import of Korean-American churches: "Without them, for example, a communication with our second generation will not be possible."[40] Korean-American churches tend to be conservative, evangelical churches. But their religious Christian conservatism is matched by their conservatism about Korean culture, interestingly enough. When Korean-Americans leave the Korean-American church, they are not only leaving Christianity. They are in fact leaving the only real connection to Korean culture and the Korean-American community available to them as an institution in America. Time is still too early to tell what kind of impact this will have on individuals, the Korean-American community, and the larger American society as a whole.

But the separation from Christianity was not the only reaction caused by 9/11. 9/11 created another extremist reaction among Koreans. Whereas some Koreans chose to abandon Christianity altogether and the only Korean communal center available to them, some Koreans became more aggressively conservative as Christians and came to thrust themselves more and more aggressively into the Korean cultural center of the Korean-American church. This radicalized element of Korean-American Christianity invited more Fundamentalist Christian preaching and teaching on the Bible. Thus, it became more and more possible to hear Korean pastors preach from the pulpit against alcohol consumption and dancing. Korean clergy who had been moderate in their preaching tended to become more Fundamentalist. And churchgoers followed this trend with a snowballing effect. Thus, in the past, they may have been willing to overlook certain things like drinking among their church-going friends, now Korean-American laity has taken on almost a witch-hunting stance towards those who engage in drinking, gambling, or dancing. For many Korean-American

---

[40] Lee, "Called to be Pilgrims," p. 65.

churches in Los Angeles, for instance, drinking came to be equated with being a non-Christian. If you drank alcohol, you could not be a Christian. Such a Fundamentalist position came to dominate the popular Korean Christian discourse since 9/11.

Such Fundamentalist trend is not only among the older generation of Korean-Americans. Many Korean-American teenagers and college students came to adopt aggressively Fundamentalist positions. Formerly evangelical Christian groups became Fundamentalist. Thus, it would not be surprising for University of California at Berkeley Korean Christians to say that a person who was not willing to take the bus for 40 minutes to go to a conservative church was not a Christian at all. A person who drinks cannot be a Christian. This kind of Fundamentalist Christian discourse came to dominate formerly moderate settings like UC Berkeley and UCLA among Christian campus organizations (such as the Korean Campus Crusade for Christ, Student For Christ (SFC), and Korean Christian Fellowship) and church groups.

Some have complained that there was a legalistic dualism developing among some of these Fundamentalist Christians. Korean-Americans who emphasized that a person who did not take a bus 40 minutes to go to a Bible-believing church was not a Christian were often caught not being able to live up to the Fundamentalist Christian standards they set for their communities. Thus, the bars were set aggressively high and the communities which established those rules often were seen as not observing those rules. This worked to create a greater dichotomy within the Korean-American community. Korean-Americans who left the church used this discrepancy to justify their departure from Christianity. Those in the Fundamentalist Christian communities emphasized Fundamentalist Christian rules more to ensure that the violators come into line with the rules set for the Christian community.

Before 9/11, Korean-American Christians tended to exist in a broadly evangelical setting, but those days ended with 9/11. Many Korean teenagers left the Korean-American church and Christianity altogether. Those who remained in the church did not know what to do and reacted by going in the opposite direction of Fundamentalist Christianity. The dichotomized trend is continuing in the Korean-American community. It seems that the trend will not stop in the foreseeable future.

In terms of loyalty to America, this present-day reality has had two divergent results. Those who tended toward Fundamentalist Christianity became increasingly loyal to the USA as a country. It is not surprising to find those who remained in Christianity joining the FBI, CIA and applying to West Point and the US Naval Academy and enlisting in ROTC programs. Christianity has been identified with the USA in Korean-American churches for a longtime, so this Korean-American popular perception enmeshed in the collective psyche is the reason for such aggressive acts of loyalty to the USA. Of course, white evangelical Christians will be the first ones to tell them that America is not a Christian nation. As Rev. John MacArthur of the famous Grace Community Church in California says, America is not the Kingdom of Christ; Kingdom of Christ is in Heaven. For Korean-American Christians, this is an oxymoron. America is a Christian nation, so to be a Christian means to be loyal to the United States of America.

Whereas Korean-American Christians becoming more and more Fundamentalist Christians grew more and more loyal to the USA, those Korean-American who left the church went the opposite direction. Typically, Korean-Americans who left the church also silently renounced their allegiance to the USA. Thus, many Korean-Americans who left the Korean-American church ally themselves with China politically as well as philosophically. Whereas Korean-American Christians tend to be anti-China and pro-America, Korean-Americans who left the Christian church tend to be aggressively pro-China and tacitly anti-America. In an unprecedented way, many Korean-Americans are drifting into socialist and communist ideologies right now, whereas such a phenomenon was practically non-existent before 9/11. Thus, we have a situation where some Korean-Americans will not think twice about betraying the USA to a foreign power because they do not see any identity with America. They have left Christianity and with it their fundamental loyalty to the United States of America, which they believed were founded on Christian principles, which they left behind. Thus, whereas it would have been impossible to see a Korean-American abet China or North Korea in attacking USA before 9/11, now there is a young generation of Korean-Americans who despise Christianity and all that is related to it who may find themselves allying themselves with China or North Korea, lands which they have never even visited. Of course, the trend is relatively new; less than 5 years old, so it is difficult to say with certainty. But the trend away from pro-USA and toward pro-China is continuing among this group of Korean-American youth and the real significance will be felt in the next 5-10 years.

Heerak Christian Kim

Chapter 2:
"Korean-American Youth in the General American Social Context"

To better understand the recent phenomenon of Korean-American youths being pulled in two opposite directions, it is important to examine the experience of Korean-Americans in the general American context. Korean-American youth are caught between two worlds. The majority of the Korean-Americans who are teenagers or in college have parents who see themselves predominantly as "Korean." This is not to say that they do not have American citizenships. In fact, the majority of the parents of Korean-American youth today will be American citizens. And many of the parents would have lived in America for over 10 years. Many would have been in the United States for the majority of their lives. Still, the current reality is that the majority of the Korean-American parents of Korean-American youth would were born in Korea. Since the United States of America does not allow immigration from North Korea, this means that they are from South Korea.

The fact that the parents of the Korean-American youth today view themselves as "Korean" is significant because it relates to their primary reference point. They do not see America as their land or culture, fundamentally, although they may say so to their white friends. Furthermore, Korean-American parents raise their children with a strong Korean-centric bias.[41] What this means is

---

[41] Sunok Chun Pai, "The Changing Role of Korean-Americans," *The Emerging Generation of Korean-Americans*, eds. Ho-Youn Kwon and Shin Kim (Seoul: Kyung Hee University Press, 1993, pp. 215-224), p. 218.

that they will try consciously to raise their children as "Koreans" and not as "Americans." This sentiment is best encapsulated in the comment by Sang-O Rhee: "What we desire most is that the second generation should identify with the Korean society in America and Korea and develop positive attitudes toward them."[42] For most Korean-American parents who follow this general trend in the Korean-American community, they will use "American" and "white" interchangeably. Thus, they may say, "Do not marry an American." This does not mean that their children should not marry an American citizen. They are all American citizens and most of the Koreans in their churches will be American citizens. What their parents mean by this is: "Do not marry a white person."

If one talks to a Korean-American youth in high school, one will notice that he will use the same category as his parents.[43] Thus, if you ask him what nationality he is, he will answer "Korean," although he was born in America and holds the United States citizenship. His Korean-American parents have provided him with his reference points and often this reference point remains in place throughout high school. Most Korean-American youth do not question the reference point until much later in high school or in college. Since they are living with their parents and are influenced daily by their parents' reference points and social definitions, they rarely question them. Thus, even in the Korean-American youth culture, saying "American" is like saying "white."[44] Thus, a Korean-American youth saying, "I will marry an American," means that they will marry a white person. They

---

[42] Sang-O Rhee, "The Leaders of 21st Century Korean Communities in America: The Role of Second Generation Education," *The Korean-American Community: Present and Future*, eds. Tae-Hwan Kwak and Seong Hyong Lee (Seoul: Kyungnam University Press, 1991, pp. 157-179), p. 172.
[43] Shinyoung Lee, *Impact of Ethnic Identity on Psychological Well-Being among Korean-Americans in the United States* (Ph.D. dissertation for the School of Social Welfare of State University of New York at Albany, 2001), pp. 4, 22.
[44] In the African-American culture, preference for white culture is equated with a negative attitude toward one's own group (Lee, *Impact of Ethnic Identity*, p. 8).

will distinguish non-whites from "American."[45] Thus, a Korean-American youth who is dating a Mexican-American who is a third generation American in Los Angeles will not say, "I am dating an American." He will say, "I am dating a Mexican." He will typically not say, "Mexican-American" just as he will not typically say, "Korean-American." A typical Korean-American teenager in Los Angeles will not qualify an ethnic identity with the word "American" attached at the end. It may be due to linguistic laziness, but more likely, it is due to a social convention that he is used to. Interestingly enough, Mexican-Americans do not refer to themselves as Mexican-American but with the simple designation "Mexican." [46] Like the Korean-American community, Mexican-Americans mean "white," when they call someone "American." The only community that consciously uses the hyphenated identity marker is the African-American community. But this is a conscious process born of many years of slavery and the civil rights movement.

Today, most of the some estimated 1.7 million Korean-Americans are located in the Greater Los Angeles area (Los Angeles, Anaheim, and all the little cities surrounding them). Some estimate that up to 1.3 million Koreans live in this area, leaving only about 800,000 Koreans spread out across the United States of America. Most Korean-Americans live in and around big cities, so biggest Korean-American communities outside of the Greater Los Angeles area are Chicago, New York, Atlanta, Baltimore, and Philadelphia. But because the Korean-American community has many professionals, they are spread out evenly in rural areas which require their professional services (such as doctors, nurses, engineers, etc.). The majority of Korean-Americans live a middle class existence and the majority of Korean-Americans have college de-

---

[45] Lee, *Impact of Ethnic Identity*, p. 36.
[46] See R. Buriel and D. Cardoza, "Mexican American Ethnic Labeling: An Intrafamilial and Intergenerational Analysis," *Ethnic Identity: Formation and Transmission among Hispanics and Other Minorities*, eds. M. Bernal and G. Knight (Albany: SUNY Press, 1993, pp. 197-210).

grees. In fact, it would not be wrong to say that the greatest value in the Korean community is education. This is the case regardless of religion, social background, educational level of parents, economic considerations, etc. This is due to the heavily Confucian nature of Korean culture which emphasizes education as the highest societal value after human relationships.

Korean-Americans tend to live in neighborhoods with a good school system, so there is a tendency to find Korean-Americans near each other as they individually gravitate toward good school districts. Korean-Americans, unlike other Asian-Americans, have no problem living among non-Koreans. In fact, many Korean-Americans prefer living among non-Koreans. They have their regular Korean contact at the Korean-American church, which usually holds at least three meetings per week (Sunday morning, Wednesday night, and Friday night). Many Korean churches have a meeting every day, such as early morning prayer meetings, and not a small number go to church on a daily basis. Because there is a channel to meet Koreans on a regular basis, living closely with other Korean-Americans is not an issue. In contrast, Chinese-Americans live in pockets of Chinese-American communities. Chinese-Americans socialize purely along ethnic lines and not on religious lines. Thus, a normative type of neighborhood association operates. Most Chinese-Americans do not go to church, and they do not have the church as their primary center of association with other Chinese-Americans. The case is completely different for Korean-Americans. Korean-Americans, during the whole course of American immigration history, have centralized the Korean-American church as the primary place to meet Korean friends.

Although Korean-Americans live in neighborhoods that may be predominantly white, Korean-Americans do not normally associate with their neighbors. Some white individuals resent this because in white suburbs, there is a certain expectation of neighborliness as defined along white American lines. Because Koreans are not white and most do not know what is expected of them, they often offend their white neighbors without intending to.[47] Often, Koreans view with suspicion when white neighbors come over with welcome fruit baskets or holiday gifts. It is not the kind of neighborliness practiced in the Korean culture. The way neighbors associate with each other in Korea is different from the way white America operates. In the Confucian Korean culture, there is no obligation to one's neighbor. They just happen to be living next to where you live. The Confucian system does not regard neighbors as friends. This stands in stark contrast to white suburbia. Neighbors are expected to be friends. Such an expectation in Korea would be considered socially unacceptable. Neighbors can become friends, but this is rare in Korea. One has one's set of friends and family members. Confucian guidelines have strict dictates to guide these relationships. But a neighbor is a stranger in the Confucian system.

Although the children of Korean-American parents who operate mostly from the "Korean" matrix may develop an American-centered perspective and point of view, more often than not, Korean-American youth subscribe to the similar social vision of their parents, which is based on the Confucian system. Thus, it would not be surprising to see Korean-American youth associating primarily with other Korean-Americans from church, rather than friends from the neighborhood or even white friends from school. Thus, during the summer time, Korean-American youth go to Korean-American Christian camps with their church friends, have heightened church activities, and some even see church friends on a daily basis. In contrast, Korean-American youth often neglect their white friends during summer vacation months and do not think seriously about the fact that they are being neglected by their white friends during the summer vacation time. Like their parents, most Korean-American youths today predominantly associate with

---

[47] Won Moo Hurh, "Comparative Study of Korean Immigrants in the United States: A Typology," *Korean Christian Scholars Journal* 2 (Spring, 1977, pp. 60-99), p. 94.

their Korean-American friends and do not consider their neighborhood youngsters as "good" friends. Of course, exceptions exist, but these exceptions prove the rule. This is the reality across America, and not just in the Korean-concentrated Greater Los Angeles area.

But socialization in the context of the Korean-American family is not the only reason why Korean-American youths of today have predominantly Korean-American friends. Many Korean-American youths would say that they are intentionally or unintentionally driven in that direction. Some will even say that it is not a matter of choice but of necessity. To understand what they mean, we should look at the pattern of Korean-American socialization in the American context. Tong-He Koh identifies five stages of development: Conformity, Dissonance, Resistance and Immersion, Introspection, and Synergetic Articulation and Awareness.[48] At the Conformity Stage, the minority individual seeks wholehearted preference for the dominant culture. The first stage is followed by Dissonance stage when the minority individual encounters traumatic events tied to her identity as a person of color. This experience is followed by the Resistance and Immersion stage, where the person of color completely rejects the dominant culture and fully endorses minority held views. The third stage is followed by the Introspection stage. At this stage, the individual questions the rigid position against dominant society held during the Resistance and Immersion stage and also the wholesale endorsement of the minority position. This fourth stage is followed by the Synergetic Articulation and Awareness Stage. At this fifth and final stage, the person of color takes a logical step from the fourth stage and makes "objective" decisions regarding the positives and negatives of the dominant and the minority groups. Korean-American youth

---

[48] Ton-He Koh, "Ethnic Identity: The Impact of Two Cultures on the Psychological Development of Korean-American Adolescents," *The Emerging Generation of Korean-Americans*, eds. Ho-Youn Kwon and Shin Kim (Seoul: Kyung Hee University Press, 1993, pp. 29-46), p. 31.

generally follow these stages, but more frequently the final stage entails embracing the Korean side over against the dominant identity.

Many Korean-American youths testify that the majority of their friends in elementary school tend to be non-Koreans. But as they grow older, they tend to gravitate toward Koreans. So, in junior high school, the same youth will have more Korean friends. Typically, a Korean-American youth will have at least 50 per cent of their friends being Koreans in high school even if they live in a neighborhood where there are no Koreans. The Korean-American church will supply them with Korean friends.[49] And once they can drive, they can drive their cars to meet Korean friends in other neighborhoods or at church. The pattern continues for college in the sense that the same Korean person will have a greater concentration of Korean friends in college. Thus, it is possible for a Korean youth to have no Korean friends in elementary school. They may see their Korean "friends" in church only on Sundays, but spend 6 days with white friends. In junior high, there is a greater possibility that there are Koreans in school because junior high school tends to be bigger and covers a wider geographical area. Thus, he may add a Korean friend whom he sees regularly at school. But still most of his friends whom he sees on a daily basis are white. When he goes to high school, he may make more Korean friends. Again, high school covers a greater geographical area than junior high schools.

It is in the time of puberty that Korean-American teenagers tend to ask conscious questions about their identity. Thus, as they are searching for their identity, they tend to gravitate toward Koreans, if there are Koreans in high school. By the time college comes around, there will be many Koreans. Most Koreans go to college and they tend to go to colleges that are academically re-

---

[49] June Ha, "1.5 and 2.0 Generation of Korean Women," *The Emerging Generation of Korean-Americans*, eds. Ho-Youn Kwon and Shin Kim (Seoul: Kyung Hee University Press, 1993, pp. 225-235), p. 234.

spected. Thus, Koreans tend to gravitate toward certain types of colleges, which means that there will be a concentration of Koreans in these colleges. And there are Korean student associations and Korean Christian Bible studies for Korean-American students to make Korean-American friends. Thus, a guy who may have had only one or two Korean friends in high school will most likely end up having majority of his friends being Korean-Americans in college. Anyone who has observed the social behavior of Korean-Americans in college will know this to be an absolute truth. The majority of Korean-American college students have Korean-Americans as their primary friends. Only a minority – even less than 10 per cent – will have mostly non-Korean friends in college.

When asked about why they do this, Korean-American youth will point to rejection by white Americans.[50] Rejection comes in various forms, but these are the most common: name calling, estrangement, and pro-active rejection. First of all, let us discuss the name calling. One will be hard-pressed to find a Korean who has not been called a "Chink."[51] It is a part of the Korean-American normative experience. Korean-Americans are called "Chink" by people who hate them in school. They can even be called this in the street by some strangers. Even their friends in a state of anger may call them this. In some rare cases, Koreans report being called this by teachers or school administrators. Whether the name calling happened in a hostile setting or not, the end result is the same. It raises self-consciousness and questions regarding one's identity. It is safe to assume that most Korean-American youths today are American-born. That is because of the nature of Korean-American history. The greatest concentration of Korean immigrants came in the 1960s and 1970s.

What this means is that the majority of Korean-American youths will not have a Korean accent. They would have received

---

[50] Lee, *Impact of Ethnic Identity*, p. 25.
[51] Andrew Sung Park, *Racial Conflict and Healing: An Asian-American Theological Perspective* (Maryknoll: Orbis Books, 1996), p. 39.

all of their education in the United States from nursery or kindergarten. Many of them may appear more "American" than a white person in terms of socialization. These Korean-American youths should theoretically have no problem with adaptation and acculturation.[52] However, the problem is with color. No matter how much a Korean-American youth will try, he will not be able to escape his color. Although this is true and many Koreans go through the same process on an individual level, the problem for the Korean-American community is that there is not a color discourse like there is in the African-American community. It is a truism within the African-American community that they will be mistreated because of their color. This self-awareness may, in part, be due to their personal experiences. But more than the personal experience, the self-awareness about this issue is borne out of communal discourse and intellectualization regarding this issue among Afircan-American leaders, whose message filters down to the least educated via social channels, like the family or the church.

In contrast, the Korean-American community does not have a highly developed discourse on color and its impact on the Korean-American community and Korean-American individuals. A part of the reason is that the Korean-American immigration history is relatively young.[53] Furthermore, majority of Korean-Americans are immigrants from post-Civil Rights movements. Thus, Korean-Americans are, by in large, not impacted by color discourse that came out during the civil rights movement. Furthermore, Korean-Americans tend to be oriented toward the sciences and math, rather than humanities and the arts. Because there is less concern with literature and philosophy within the Korean-American community, color discourse which requires these tools has been slow to take hold. The lack of developed academic and popular discourse on color and Korean-American identity has forced most Korean-Americans to live the same process individually without the help

---

[52] Lee, *Impact of Ethnic Identity*, p. 26.
[53] Lee, *Impact of Ethnic Identity*, p. 92.

of enlightened explanation. Thus, Korean-American youths are hit from the behind in regards to their color. They never expected to be discriminated because of their color, because neither their parents nor their community leaders warned them about this. In contrast, a typically African-American youth would have been warned about the color issue both by his parents and his church or another African-American community organization.

Being caught off guard without any expectation of a strike can be destabilizing for the Korean-American youth. And often, Korean-American youths struggle and fail to get back on their feet, when a color-generated issue hits them. Furthermore, because they have not been given enough information to understand what is happening to them, they may blame themselves when they are not at fault.[54] When it is their color that is bringing down the attack, they may think that it is something to do with their personality or something personal to them.[55] The tendency to blame oneself rather than the unfair situation of color dynamics cause personal problems where there should be none. When Korean-American youths understand that they are not personally to be blamed for the name calling, then they can develop more healthily. It is not because they did anything wrong but it is because of the color of their skin that they are being called "Chinks." Furthermore, if they understand that this is a part of a social problem that existed for a long time, they can understand that the name calling is the result of not conscious or active hatred per se, but rather a socialized process name callers are following.

I remember hearing from my sister that a white guy who used to tease her the most ended up marrying an Asian (Vietnamese-American). He used to give my sister a tough time by calling her "egg roll" and other Asian food items. Obviously, it does not sound as bad as calling someone a "Chink." But it is like calling an African-American a "water buffalo." It is meant to be racially

---

[54] Lee, *Impact of Ethnic Identity*, pp. 37-38.
[55] Koh, "Ethnic Identity," p. 36.

derogatory and in quality no different from being called a "Chink" or "Nigger." He knew that he was using the term derogatorily to an Asian. Of course, it would have been tempting to call him a racist and dismiss the whole issue as unnatural. But the fact is, my sister is a person of color, as I am. In fact, the first thing anyone will notice about my sister and me is that we are Asians. Our color is our identity mark. And the color is an issue for most people. Just because others remained silent as this guy called my sister an "egg roll" does not mean that they were not thinking about it or that they themselves had not called an Asian an "egg roll" behind their backs. Furthermore, when they told their parents about the incident, most of the families probably had a good laugh about it. To white Americans, being called an egg roll does not sound serious. Perception is in the eye of the beholder. What sounds racist for Asians does not sound racist for non-Asians. It's just a natural human thing.

    Understanding the color discourse can give Korean-American youth a more grounded perspective on color and the reaction of whites (whether Jewish, Christian, or other) to the people of color. This will minimize a reactionary response of "white hatred" or resentment born out of assumption that they truly hate the person. Often, name calling is a part of a socialized process rather than an active act of hatred. If, in fact, this guy hated Asians, it is difficult to see how he could have married a Vietnamese-American. In fact, it would not be surprising to find his family, at least initially, objecting to him marrying an Asian-American. But he went through with the marriage and now he is happily married. In high school, he gave my sister the most difficult time. It would have been easy to jump to the conclusion that he is a racist and make a big issue out it. My sister did not do this although she was hurt by what was said. And they were able to become friends. The fact that she understood color dynamics helped her to have a balanced perspective on the white society. Her best friend to this day is white, although the majority of her friends are Korean-Americans.

Currently, there is hardly any color discourse in the Korean-American community, and that is a tragedy. That is not to say that there are not good books written by Korean-American scholars on the issue. Some do exist, but these have failed to impact the Korean-American community. Most Korean-American churches ignore the issue of color,[56] and in this regard, Korean-American churches are completely different from African-American churches, most of which will deal with the color issue because it is important to the community and because they understand the implications of it on the individual in the context of the larger American society. There is a greater assimilation of African-Americans in the US society than there is for Korean-Americans. Korean-American communities often can function without white communities and often intentionally stay away from white communal associations and greater American contextual associations. The case is different with the African-American community. Although African-American individuals may not associate actively with the white community, African-American community as such is always in negotiation with the white community at large. The African-American community is very active in politics and in social movements. Every local and state government agency has significant African-American presence and involvement, where there are African-Americans to be found. In contrast, Korean-Americans tend to shy away from government organizations and social organizations on local and state levels. Most Korean-American churches do not see their representation of Korean-Americans in the white society as one of their obligations to the Korean-American people. This stands in stark contrast to the African-American church and its self perception and mission.

Because of the lack of social programs and structures to educate the Korean-American community about the effects of color on the Korean-American individual and Korean-American communities, Korean-American youths are left not only to fend for

---

[56] Park, *Racial Conflict and Healing*, p. 93.

themselves but also to make sense of their experience as Korean-Americans along the color spectrum in the American society. It is not just the name calling that gives them a sense of deep rejection – which becomes for them a difficult puzzle to solve without communal guidance. They have to struggle to understand social ostracization as a phenomenon.

Many Korean-American youths experience some kind of social ostracization during the course of their puberty. The most common form of social ostracization is their white friends "dropping out." What this means is that white friends who were best buddies in elementary school days suddenly stop being friends when they go to junior high school. The Korean-American youth notices that soon her white friends only have white friends. But she is not sure what is going on. It is difficult enough going through puberty. She may start to blame herself and think that she did something wrong to deserve the boot. But what is happening is that this is a part of the socialization process based on color. She was not at fault in any way. She is a Korean-American and the color dynamics overtook her white friends, who caved in to the white socialization process that inherently and subconsciously favors exclusion of the people of color.

It is difficult to call her friend a racist. And calling her that will not help in any way. A better way to understand the phenomenon is to study the social dynamics based on color. You cannot call a guy racist because he prefers black women but do not like Hispanic women. Most guys have a type of girl they like. Some guys like brunette women; some guys like blondes. Not everything should be seen as racist. People have preferences. In the same way, without consciously thinking about it, color dynamics in the socialization process may impact a white American friend to abandon her friendship with her elementary school friend, who is Korean-American. It is important to understand that the white friend is in the process of understanding herself as well and is going through deep changes during her own puberty years. It should not be assumed that she is a racist. But more importantly as far as the Korean-American youth is considered, she should not blame herself for losing her friend. It is not like they are in their thirties and forties and her friend decides to dump her for being Korean. They are both in their teenage years and they are both trying to find themselves. Understanding the reality of color dynamics in socialization will help the Korean-American youth cope with rejection and not blame herself for what may not be so abnormal in the context of the color patterns of the American society. Korean-American leaders can minimize psychological and individual damage to Korean-American youths by helping them understand the color dynamics in the American society.

Besides the name calling and the social ostracization, Korean-American youths may experience pro-active rejection. By pro-active rejection, I am referring more to the dating scene. Like most teenagers, Korean-American youths will try to pursue relationships. Of course, Korean-American parents and the church can discourage dating in teenage years. But they cannot assume that they will necessarily be discouraged to date because dating is such a serious reality in the American society. And many Korean-American youths try to date. More often than not, Korean-American teenagers try to go out with white teenagers. Since the majority of the teenagers in their high school are white, this would be natural. More often than not, they will experience rejection.

This is actually quite "normal" given the reality of the color dynamics in the American context. However, because there is not sufficient discussion in Korean-American church youth groups regarding color dynamics, most Korean-Americans experiencing rejection on the romantic side will assume that there is something wrong with them or unlikable about them personally. It is easy to develop low self-esteem and doubt one's personality or character as the result of a rejection by someone a Korean-American teen has a serious crush on. But such personal blaming of oneself would not be necessary if he were aware of the color dynamics. It is possible that the girl rejected him because she just does not like his personality, but it is also possible that color dynamics weighed in on her decision. The important thing is that the Korean-American youth must be aware of the possibility that it could be due to color dynamics because this is a serious consideration and a possibility. What is needed in the Korean-American community is giving Korean-American youths a full set of information regarding the American society and the color dynamics which historically impacted the American society and the people of color so that it can help Korean-American youths wade through personal difficulties of rejection they will encounter in their life. They need not assume that they are personally at fault or that it was their personal inadequacy that caused the rejection. It may be the case but it may not be. More likely than not, color dynamics played some role, however minute.

The fact is that most Korean-Americans experience all three forms of rejection (name calling, social ostracization, and pro-active rejection) in their teenage years by white teenagers. Whatever their take on the rejection, the end result is that it drives Korean-Americans toward other Korean-Americans.[57] Sang-O Rhee describes the tumultuous process: "First, the children attempt to identify with the mainstream society and feel comfortable with it. Second, after a while with mainstream identity, they feel some disharmony and conflict with their mainstream identity. Third, they tend to reject the mainstream identity and to indulge in their own ethnic identity."[58] It is like "misery wants company." Most Korean-Americans experience the same kinds of rejection. Although it is never really talked about openly, everyone in the Korean-American youth community knows that this is going on. It is a part of their regular experience. So, without talking about it, Korean-American youth tend to gravitate toward each other with every passing year. This process reaches its climax in college. When one goes to Harvard or Yale, one will see that most Korean-Americans will have their meal with other Asian-Americans.

---

[57] Lee, *Impact of Ethnic Identity*, p. 97. Park, *Racial Conflict and Healing*, p. 94.
[58] Rhee, "The Leaders of 21st Century Korean Communities in America," p. 172.

There is a *de facto* segregation of whites and Asians at Harvard and Yale. This is the case with all American colleges, regardless of academic prestige.

In many cases, the process of rejection is most pronounced in college. Although most Korean-Americans have "learned their lesson" and find Korean-American friends and nice Koreans to date, there are Korean-Americans who pursue dreams of assimilation in college. More often than not, such efforts end up in sadness.[59] Let me give you an example of a friend of mine at the University of Pennsylvania. His parents are both doctors and he grew up in Iowa, after being born in the USA. So, he is one of the most assimilated Asian-Americans one will meet. To add to the assimilation, he went to the most elite boarding school in America, Phillips Exeter Academy, which cost more than attending many colleges in the USA. He developed many elite friends there who were white. In fact, he came to the University of Pennsylvania with his best friend from Exeter, who is white. In the freshman year, he spent a lot of time with his best friend from his high school, who was also his freshman roommate. But starting with his sophomore year, his roommates were all Asians –Asian-Americans and Asians from Asia. More and more, he started seeing less of his white friends and more of his Asian-American friends.

After graduating with a near 4.0 from the University of Pennsylvania, he went to work for a prestigious consulting firm in New York. His effort to date white women all failed as did his efforts in that regard in college. Of course, he had a very high taste, but given his qualifications and who he was, none of these white women would have rejected him if he were white. But he is not; he is an Asian-American. After a few years of working in New York, he went to Stanford to take an MBA and started his own internet company. He fell in love with a Chinese-American

---

[59] David S. Rue, "Depression and Suicidal Behavior among AsianWhiz Kids," *The Emerging Generation of Korean-Americans*, eds. Ho-Youn Kwon and Shin Kim (Seoul: Kyung Hee University Press, 1993, pp. 91-106), p. 102.

woman and married her. At Stanford, he did not even consider dating a non-Asian. Most of his closest friends remained Asian since his PENN days.

His case highlights the plight of the Korean-American. My friend is not Korean-American but most Asian-Americans experience similar social rejection by whites since Asian-Americans look alike. Of course, it is only a plight if one seeks assimilation. But the fact is, this friend of mine is the most polished Asian-American one will ever meet. The fact that he did not receive social acceptance by whites makes it nearly impossible for any other Asian-Americans to receive social acceptance. Of course, he never once complained about the situation, but I know that it weighed heavily in his heart. In the end, he opted to reject the white society and entrenched himself socially in the Asian-American community. This is what happens to most qualified Asian-Americans. In fact, some would say that this is expected of qualified Asian-Americans.

Let me give you another example of social rejection experienced in college by Asian-Americans. I was talking with a Vietnamese-American guy from San Jose who was studying for his business degree at the University of California at Berkeley, and we came to the topic of Asians and the white society. He said that most of his friends were white and that he belonged to mostly white fraternity at Berkeley. He looked a bit unhappy as we started to talk about the issue, so I flat out came out and told him that I can predict what he is going through at Berkeley. He wanted to know how I would know. I told him that Asian-Americans experience similar patterns throughout the United States of America, regardless of which state. There were exceptions, but these exceptions proved the rule. I knew this based on my research.

He became quite interested at that point and wanted to hear what I had to say. I told him that most Asians joining white fraternities experience the same kind of awakening at some point in their fraternity life. They may not experience name calling because that tends to decrease as one moves up the grade. So, in high school there would be less name calling than in junior high school. In college, it is difficult to find name calling. But what does exist in college are the other two forms of rejection: social ostracization and pro-active rejection. I told him that the most common form of rejection that Asian-American frat boys experience is pro-active rejection by white women.

He was interested in this topic and asked me to explain. To help him understand, I drew up a scenario. In fraternity, there is a lot of drinking. He agreed. And in frat parties, many people get drunk – both men and women. There is generally some kind of dancing. Like most men, Asian-American frat boys will approach white women whom they find attractive. In many cases, these white women will be drunk. Often, frat guys see it as their advantage that the women are drunk. But I told the Vietnamese-American guy that, more often than not, the fact that the white women are drunk will bring Asian-American men a rude awakening.

When these sorority girls were sober, they had their social guard up, so they treated Asian-American fraternity guys nicely. But when they became intoxicated, they dropped their social guard and political correctness. On the dance floor, when they are drunk, they may allow white fraternity guys to be more aggressive than when they were sober. Their inhibition – in this case, sexual inhibition – was down. But just as their sexual inhibition was down because of being drunk, their other inhibitions may be dropped as well, such as inhibition attached to political correctness. Thus, when they were sober they might have hidden their disdain for Asian-American men, when their inhibition was gone, they would allow their dislike for Asian-Americans show.

Thus, when white fraternity boys would approach them, they would let them touch them or draw closer to them. But in the same state of intoxication where inhibitions were dropped, the same girl will put up a fight or push away an Asian-American frat boy who would do the same. It can be argued that it was not because he was Asian-American, but this argument fails upon closer observation. A white sorority girl who is drunk may be approached by more than one frat guy for a dance. It will generally be observed that she will allow access into her personal space for all white fraternity guys while not allowing Asian-American frat guy the same kind of access to her personal space. She is not consciously doing this because she is drunk. Asian-American guys, no matter how dense they are, will understand sooner or later that the pro-active rejection is due to the fact that they are Asian-American. Especially at a place like UC Berkeley, this would be more keenly felt. To this, the Vietnamese-American guy nodded. He had experienced something like that.

Of course, anyone who has studied the issues of color knows that there is a world of literature out there about the issue. Men of Color have been portrayed as sexual predators in literature and in popular understanding. *To Kill A Mockingbird* is a conscious social critique of this reality in America. Thus, it is understandable that being socialized in the American context to see men of color as sexual predators or violent individuals, white women will react based on this social stereotype of the men of color. Of course, if she were sober, she may not have acted in such a hostile manner against Asian-Americans. Whatever may have been her intention or lack of awareness, the fact is that Asian-American frat boys experience pro-active rejection in college. And this drives them towards the Asian-American community as well. Rejection is a fact of the Asian-American experience and those who have not learned the lesson to retreat into the Asian-American community will experience many painful forms of rejection – often, not intended maliciously to be painful. However, after all the self-exploration and education, Asian-Americans who are trying to assimilate have gained a heightened sense of understanding and analysis of society, social structures, and human relations. Thus, rejection looms far larger and more seriously than it would have before being enlightened in college through education and pro-active and critical thinking.

What all this points to is the reality that Asian-Americans understand that they are outside of the normative white American society. The majority of Asian-Americans understand this by the time they reach 30 years old. Probably less than 1 per cent of the Asian-American community members feel otherwise. Thus, while participating in economic, political, and social life of the United States, Asian-Americans participate as Asian-American individuals in the context of being members of the Asian-American community. In other words, Asian-Americans do not participate in American economic, political, and social life as generic Americans, like a typical white person, without regards to their relationship to the Asian-American community. Most white Americans who have Asian-American friends and understand their social world will be able to relate to this reality. This reality is ubiquitous in the American society, regardless of which region of the United States.

What does this mean? Asian-Americans are a society within the American society. It is a fully self-contained, independently functioning social structure, not dependent on the general American society. This means that at any point, Asian-Americans can abandon their allegiance to the USA. In fact, most of them are not a part of the American society at large, regardless of whether they are janitors or a vice president of an international corporation. Their primary social matrix will undoubtedly be Asian-American or Asian.

This is true of Korean-Americans as well. Most Korean-American youths do not have an allegiance to white America. In fact, there is a deep resentment against white America by most Korean-Americans. There is a greater resentment and dislike of white America among Korean-Americans born in the USA than Korean-Americans born in Korea. Whereas Korean-Americans born in Korea tend to be pro-Korean, they tend not to be specifically anti-American. In contrast, Korean-Americans born in America tend to be pro-Korean via being anti-American. And by anti-American, we mean anti-white American. The reason for this is clear. Most Korean-Americans, growing up in white middle class neighborhoods, going to elite colleges, have experienced rejection by white

Americans, despite their effort and their skills and hard-earned education. There is resentment borne out of personal experiences.

The only thing that keeps Korean-Americans loyal to the United States has been the perception that America is a Christian nation. Since most Korean-Americans tend to be evangelical Christians, they value their Christian identity over all else, including their Korean identity. Thus, the perception that America is a Christian nation has kept a certain segment of the Korean-American population very loyal and patriotic to America. But 9/11 and ensuing opening up of the American society along multi-religious lines have disgusted evangelical Christian sensibilities. Thus, even evangelical Christians are losing their historic loyalty to the United States. Whereas white American patriotism is built on some nebulous idea of freedom, Korean loyalty to America was built largely on the notion – however misguided – that America is a Christian nation. The basis for patriotism is completely different. Most Korean-Americans cannot feel patriotism to white America, which they feel disenfranchises them on a daily basis and imposes a glass ceiling over them. Hardly any evangelical Korean-American Christian will deny having experienced rejection and discrimination by white America.

After 9/11 and the ensuing aggressive push for multi-religious identity, many Korean-Americans were shaken from their mistaken perception of America as a Christian nation. Many tended toward the anti-American position as a result. There was nothing to keep them from hating the white America that often rejected them and continues to reject them, especially if it stands against Christian value that Christ alone is God and King – a historical evangelical Christian theological position.

Since all Korean-Americans experience rejection by white America at some point in their life – whether done intentionally or maliciously or not – other group of Koreans who do not fall into the evangelical Christian camp certainly tend to be not very pro-America. In many cases, they tend to be aggressively anti-

America as they remember the rejection of white America on their life and in the lives of Korean-American around them they see.

Chapter 3:
"The Nature of Korean-American Christianity"

Because Christianity is so important to the Korean-American community, it is important to examine the nature of Korean-American Christianity in order to understand individual and communal identity of Korean-Americans.[60] As mentioned earlier, close to 100 per cent of Korean-American youths have been to a Korean-American church at some point in their life. Even non-Christian parents encourage their children to go to a Korean-American church to gain exposure to other Korean-American teenagers and to learn about the Korean culture. The Korean-American Church is the central social institution of the Korean-American community and the primary cultural institution for preserving and teaching Korean culture.[61] Don-Chang Lee writes: "Thus Koreans maintain their solidarity as an ethnic group, while the church provides opportunity for social interaction. In this aspect the Korean Church is a social fact and arose out of the nature of social life itself."[62] All Korean-Americans understand this reality, so even non-Christian Korean-Americans send their children to

---

[60] All studies on Korean-Americans regardless of discipline must gather data through Korean-American churches. The Korean-American church is the primary Korean-American social institution. Every book on Korean-Americans confirms this in acknowledging its indebtedness to the Korean-American church for research into Korean-Americans.

[61] Lee, *Impact of Ethnic Identity*, pp. 39-40.

[62] Don-Chang Lee, "A Study of Social Networks within Two Korean Communities in America," *The Korean Diaspora: Historical and Sociological Studies of Korean Immigration and Assimilation in North America*, ed. Hyung-Chan Kim (Santa Barbara: ABC-Clio, Inc., 1977, pp. 155-166), p. 160.

a Korean-American church even if they have objections to the Christian faith and even if they themselves do not go to church.[63]

Since the Korean-American church has gained such an undisputed power over the Korean-American community as the central Korean institution in the USA, it is not surprising that there are so many ethnically Korean churches in America.[64] Currently, there are estimated 5,000 to 7,000 Korean churches in America of all Christian denominations. Where there are a few Korean families even in the most rural America, there will be a Korean church. The saying goes that where there are two Japanese people, they will start a business. Where there are two Chinese people, they will start a Chinese restaurant. But where there are two Koreans, they will start a church. In terms of Koreans, this is absolutely true.[65] Where there are a few Koreans, there will be a Korean church. This is not only the case in America, but all the countries in the world. Visiting Korean areas of any country in the world will prove this to be an absolute fact.

It is not surprising, therefore, that there are so many Koreans pursuing the study of theology. Most of America's Christian seminaries – regardless of which Christian denomination – will have at least 20-50 per cent of their students being Koreans. This is true of seminaries of all spectra. The greatest concentration of Korean students is at Westminster Theological Seminary, Fuller Theological Seminary, and Princeton Theological Seminary.[66] The reason why Koreans tend to gravitate toward Presbyterian seminar-

---

[63] Lee, *Impact of Ethnic Identity*, p. 96.
[64] Jae Hyung Chai, "The Korean-American Community and U.S. Politics," *The Korean-American Community: Present and Future*, eds. Tae-Hwan Kwak and Seong Hyong Lee (Seoul: Kyungnam University Press, 1991, pp. 93-97), p. 95.
[65] Andrew Sung Park, *Racial Conflict and Healing: An Asian-American Theological Perspective* (Maryknoll: Orbis Books, 1996), p. 94.
[66] Yong-Choon Kim, "The Protestant Church and the Korean-American Community," *The Korean-American Community: Present and Future*, eds. Tae-Hwan Kwak and Seong Hyong Lee (Seoul: Kyongnam University Press, 1991, pp. 195-209), p. 201.

ies is that the Presbyterian Church is the biggest church in Korea. The number of Presbyterians outnumbers the total number of Roman Catholics in South Korea. In contrast, America has at most 5 million Presbyterians (of all Presbyterian denominations), whereas there are over 60 million or more Roman Catholics. The fact that the American Revolution was called "The Presbyterian Revolution" by the English at the time makes this reality significant. Whereas at the beginning of the country, the USA was predominantly Presbyterian-tending as to have the American Revolution characterized as a Presbyterian Revolution, now the USA has minimal Presbyterian influence. Some would describe Presbyterianism in America in its death throes.

    The case is completely different in Korea. American Presbyterian missionaries have been very aggressive in Korea and they have reaped the fruits of their labor. The kind of Presbyterianism represented in Korea is of the Fundamentalist kind. Yong Choon Kim describes the nature of Korean Christianity: "One of the main reasons for the rapid growth of the Korean Protestant church is that the majority of its members have been evangelical in theology and faith. They have firmly held the view that the Bible is the Word of God, have diligent study of the Bible, have been fervent in prayer, have had frequent meetings of worship, and have made diligent efforts for evangelical and missionary work."[67] In a sense, Korean Presbyterians can be equated to American Presbyterians in terms of Calvinistic theology but to the Southern Baptists in terms of their holy living emphasis. A typical Korean Presbyterian church will not allow drinking, smoking, dancing, or gambling. Korean Presbyterianism impacted Korean Christianity in a serious way, so that all the other Korean Christian denominations have a similar flavor.

    Korean churches in America are impacted by this conservative Christian trend in South Korea. Yong Choon Kim writes: "Through these frequent and diligent meetings and a strong or-

---

[67] Kim, "The Protestant Church and the Korean-American Community," p. 196.

ganization system, the Korean-American Protestant church has grown rapidly. Such a system of frequent meetings of the Korean-American church is a direct transmission of the same system and tradition of the Protestant church in Korea."[68] In fact, Korean-American churches are primarily tied to their Korean counterparts rather than to their American counterparts. Thus, a conservative Korean-American denomination will be closer to a conservative Korean denomination in South Korea, rather than a conservative American denomination in the United States. Also, Korean churches of the United Methodist Church (UMC) will be closer to Korean Methodist Church in South Korea rather than to the United Methodist Church (UMC) in America even though they are a part of the denomination in the United States.[69] The same is the case for the Presbyterian Church USA (PCUSA). Korean churches which are members of the Presbyterian Church USA (PCUSA) will be closer to Korean Presbyterian Church (Tong-Hap) or other Korean Presbyterian denominations in South Korea, rather than to the Presbyterian Church USA, even though they are member

---

[68] Kim, "The Protestant Church and the Korean-American Community," p. 196.

[69] In fact, many Korean United Methodist Church member congregations have experienced discrimination by white United Methodist Church congregations, according to Andrew Sung Park (Andrew Sung Park, *Racial Conflict and Healing: An Asian-American Theological Perspective* [Maryknoll: Orbis Books, 1996], p. 21). Andrew Sung Park criticizes the United Methodist Church (UMC): "Although Korean-American and Euro-American pastors are appointed by the same bishop of a conference, many Korean-American pastors who start new congregations have to beg fellow Euro-American pastors to rent their buildings to their congregations. They are treated as second-class pastors" (p. 21). A part of the UMC white discrimination against Korean-American pastors is due to the fact that pastors of color (Korean-Americans, Hispanic-Americans, and African-Americans) tend to be more conservative theologically than white UMC pastors. Thus, UMC discrimination against Korean pastors can be seen as twofold: based on color and on account of their more conservative theological orientation. In one sense, it is possible to say that white UMC discrimination against Korean UMC pastors is facilitated by the dominant position of white pastors in the UMC, maintained and encouraged by white UMC pastors as a collective.

churches of the Presbyterian Church USA. In this, it can be said that Korean-American Christians see themselves as a part of Korean Christianity rather than American Christianity in terms of denominational affiliation, theological leaning, loyalty, religiosity, and value for the community.[70]

This reality should not be surprising for someone who is familiar with the African-American church. It does not matter if you go to an African-Methodist-Episcopal (AME) church, which is thought to be liberal, or a Southern Baptist African-American church, the feel will be similar in the African-American congregation. In the like manner, African-American churches which are a part of the United Methodist Church (UMC) will feel a greater kinship with African-American churches and African-American denominations. In fact, African-American clergy in a given area will meet with African-American clergy and associate primarily with them across denominational and theological lines. Their African-American identity triumphs over earthly denominational affiliations. In the same way, Korean clergy in a given area will associate with Korean clergy across denominational spectra. Korean-Americans are under the mercy of the Korean-American community. This rule applies to Korean-American clergy as well as Korean-American laity. Thus, privileging an American denomination over a Korean denomination, even if theologically different, will incur the wrath of the Korean-centric Korean-American community. Korean-American clergy are aware of this, so even if they may not want to participate in the Korean-American clergy association, they will do so for the sake of survival within the Korean-American community and on account of the expectations of the Korean-American community, including their church members. Every city has an interdenominational Korean clergy association and the majority of the Korean clergy, regardless of the denomination, are members. When I was in Cambridge, I was a part of the

---

[70] Kim, "The Protestant Church and the Korean-American Community," pp. 203-204.

Cambridge Korean Theologians Association, which brought together licensed and ordained clergy in the whole city of Cambridge. There were Korean clergy of all denominations and all theological leanings. There were regular monthly meetings that were official and many met unofficially as friends on a regular basis. Korean clergy associations tend to be conservative evangelical because that is the nature of Korean Christianity. Korean-American Christianity is conservative evangelical like Korean Christianity. This is the case in Cambridge and Oxford in the United Kingdom as well.

Often, white Christians in liberal seminaries complain about Korean Christians because they think that Korean Christians are too conservative. The spectrum of conservative-liberal is completely different in the Korean community. In the Korean community, people who drink are considered liberal even if their theology is often seen as Fundamentalist or super-conservative by American mainstream Christians. Most Korean Christians judge along Fundamentalist guidelines. Thus, it is not surprising that Korean Methodist students regularly complain about Methodist seminaries in the United States. Korean Methodism has been deeply impacted by holiness movements and Korean Methodists tend to be Fundamentalists. In contrast, the United Methodist Church (UMC) represents permissiveness within American Christianity. Thus, the Claremont School of Theology and other United Methodist Church (UMC) seminaries will have religiously Jewish individuals training Christians to be clergy in the United Methodist Church (UMC) (and they have other non-believer professors). Many Korean Methodist students regularly complain about this among themselves and often condemn the seminary, even though they are students there and belong officially to the United Methodist Church (UMC). Often, white Americans do not understand why Korean Methodists are so Fundamentalist, although the Holiness Movement as a Wesleyan tradition is a part of the Methodist heritage. Most of the aggressively Fundamentalist denominations in the United States are Wesleyan and not Calvinist in their theological leaning.

It is not surprising, therefore, that many Korean students in liberal seminaries boycott the seminary and seminary programs in some way. If they do attend seminary social functions, they refuse to chat with white seminary students or other members of the seminary community because they harbor a deep-seated resentment against the seminary's liberal policy of hiring Jews and atheists to faculty positions and because they think that white students in liberal seminaries support this position. Most Koreans go to an American seminary not based on theological persuasion, but rather on historic reputation or because they are sister seminaries of the seminaries they attended in South Korea. The Korean Methodist Church (KMC) and the United Methodist Church (UMC) may be sister denominations, but they are not agreed in the majority of main theological points. For instance, Korean Methodist Seminary fired its tenured, senior professor in Christian ethics because he supported homosexuality. He did not even support homosexual ordination. He said that homosexuality should be allowed among Methodists attending church. Because of this position, he lost his faculty position which he held for decades. He is academically the most respected Christian ethics scholar in South Korea. He is well-known around the world. But for the Korean Methodist Church, his academic reputation did not matter. He was too liberal for the Korean Methodist Church.

A similar kind of experience confronted Fuller Theological Seminary's Dr. Seyoon Kim. When he became a professor at Chong-Shin Seminary, which is the denominational seminary of the biggest Korean Presbyterian denomination, he was the most famous Korean New Testament scholar around the world. A few years later, he was fired from his tenured position because of his "liberal" ideas. Fortunately, he was able to get a teaching job at Asia Center for Theological Studies (ACTS), which is a broadly evangelical seminary in South Korea, thought to be in the left side of the theological spectrum in South Korea. It was when he was teaching at ACTS that Fuller Theological Seminary, not aware of the Korean taboo on his head, recruited him to be a professor at

Fuller Theological Seminary. Fuller Theological Seminary knew of his international repute as a New Testament scholar. In the Korean context, academic excellence always takes a second seat to theological commitment to the Christian denomination of the seminary where the professor is teaching. All the Korean Christian seminaries are evangelical – most will be described as Fundamentalist Christian by an average American Christian and certainly by liberal seminaries like the Claremont School of Theology.

Although liberal seminaries in America have big concentrations of Korean students, the greatest concentration of Koreans are found in conservative seminaries. The more conservative the seminary in America, the more Korean applicants they will have. And in liberal seminaries in America, Korean students represent the most conservative element in the seminary. For example, if one surveys the Korean student population at Princeton Theological Seminary, which is renown around the world for its academic power, one will notice that Korean students are Fundamentalist Christians by Presbyterian Church USA standards. Many of them have prayer meetings at 5:30 AM or 6 AM, every day. They will prohibit drinking, smoking, or dancing. They will subscribe to a very conservative theology. Some at Princeton Theological Seminary resent the presence of Korean students at the seminary because they are the most conservative people in the seminary and there are a lot of them. Even the most liberal Korean Christian denomination is evangelical and Korean-American Christian denominations share in this conservative trend.

It is not only in seminaries that conservative Christian presence of Korean Christianity is felt. If one goes to Harvard or Yale, one will quickly note that the "Fundies" (derogatory term for "Fundamentalist Christians") are mostly Koreans. During the freshman orientation week, Christian group tables will be filled with Koreans. Many white students who are secular have come to identify Campus Crusade for Christ and InterVarsity Christian Fellowship as Korean Bible study groups because of the dominance of Korean-American students in these groups. It is not surprising to find that many Christian leaders are Koreans in the Ivy League and many other elite universities. For instance, in 1997 when my friend Rev. Billy Park was the pastor of the Brown University Church, offering Protestant Christian worship service every Sunday at the Brown University Chapel, 90 per cent of about 120 students who attended every Sunday morning were Korean-American undergraduate students of Brown University. That is practically the majority of the total population of Korean-American undergraduates at Brown University. Only about 10 per cent of the church attendance was non-Korean, divided among whites, African-Americans, and other Asians. A graduate of Wesleyan University and Princeton Theological Seminary, Rev. Billy Park was ordained in the most conservative Korean-American Presbyterian denomination (Ko-Shin), and held to a very conservative evangelical Christian position, which mirrored the theological conservatism of Korean-American undergraduate students at Brown University. Often, Korean-American youth who stay in the Christian church during college days tend to be more conservative than the older generation of Koreans and even their college pastors.[71]

What fuels the conservative Christian position of Korean-American youths who proactively confess their Christian identity? How is it that Korean-American youths often tend to be far more conservative than their youth pastor who has been to a seminary? It is interesting to note that in denominations that are liberal, such as the United Methodist Church (UMC), Korean-American youth have been known to organize and drive out youth pastors who do not conform to a Fundamentalist Christian world-view and conservative Biblical teaching. It is important to note that the conservatism in Korean-American churches is not a top-down reality. In other words, it is not because the clergy are preaching conserva-

---

[71] Robert D. Goette, "The Transformation of a First Generation Church into a Bilingual Second Generation Church," *The Emerging Generation of Korean-Americans*, eds. Ho-Youn Kwon and Shin Kim (Seoul: Kyung Hee University Press, 1993, pp. 237-251), p. 245.

tism that Korean-American church goers are conservative. Social conservatism is a part of the Korean culture, and conservative preaching merely reinforces cultural values of the Korean society passed down through the generations.

To illustrate this point, I will refer to the Korean cultural context. In the 1970s, if a Korean youth of 16 were caught smoking in South Korea, a stranger had the right to beat him up to a pulp. If his parents saw his son getting beaten up for smoking, they would thank the stranger for teaching his son an important lesson. Smoking was seen as something that the youth must not do. The same was true with drinking. If a Korean youth were caught drinking, any stranger had the social and cultural right to beat him up. It was seen as doing the Korean society a service. The same is true for youths who gambled. Although as an adult, such practices are permitted and in some contexts done excessively, the fact is that there was a societal expectation for youth. This expectation resembled Fundamentalist Christian requirements. Thus, there was a conservative social and cultural trend that was integral to the Korean society. Yong Choon Kim writes: "In contrast to the secular American society and many liberal American churches, most Korean churches emphasized authority, order, and peace in the home based on the teachings of the Bible, which are in accord with the traditional Confucian ethics in the Korean society. Through such emphasis, Korean churches have made a significant contribution to the well-being of the Korean-American society."[72] Korean Christianity merely fed this reality and extended it to include the adults as well.

Furthermore, Korean Christianity in America developed further along conservative evangelical lines because the large brunt of Korean-American immigration was in the 1960s and the 1970s.[73] The conservative social mores of this period was fixed in the Korean-American community, and it was as if time had

---

[72] Kim, "The Protest Church and the Korean-American Community," p. 198.
[73] Park, *Racial Conflict and Healing*, pp. 96-98.

stopped. As many Koreans worked 15 hour per day shifts in grocery stores or dry cleaner's, they had not time to explore other cultural realities. They knew only the mores they left behind in Korea, and it became the standard for themselves and their children. 1960s and 1970s Korea was very conservative socially as Korea tried to survive as a nation after a devastating Korean War. Christian or not, conservative cultural values ruled the Korean-American family of this period. The values passed on among their children and their children's children.

Fundamentalist Christianity merely reinforced social values that many Korean-Americans held dear. In fact, most Korean-American churchgoers expected the Christian clergy to expound these conservative positions from the pulpit. Conservative churches flourished and liberal churches withered in the Korean-American community. Even today, a typical white Christian will be shocked by the conservatism of a typical Korean-American church. Korean-American churches are so conservative that getting a Harvard degree in theology becomes a life-long liability. If a theologian gets a Ph.D. from Harvard, he must bend backwards and forwards to prove that it was not in the area of theology but in the area of history or some other non-theological discipline. The conservative Korean-American community deeply mistrusts liberal theological institutions, like Harvard, Yale, and the University of Chicago. This explains why the smallest percentage of Korean seminary students is found in these places. Getting a theological degree from these places makes one unemployable in the Korean-American church. This is just as true for a United Methodist Church (UMC) member Korean church as it is for a Southern Baptist member Korean church. For many years, Chong-Shin University threw out applications (for faculty positions) of anyone who had Harvard University anywhere in their resume for fear that it would taint their Christian faith and denominational commitments. Chong Shin University, by policy, hired Westminster Theological Seminary Ph.D. graduates to be their professors over Ph.D.'s from America's elite institutions. For them, conservative evangelical faith was the highest value, not academic reputation in the secular context. Still today, if a theologian says he received his Ph.D. from Harvard or Yale, he will struggle in the Korean-American Christian context for respect and a place of honor.

It is not surprising, therefore, that Fuller Theological Seminary, Westminster Theological Seminary, Dallas Theological Seminary, and Trinity Evangelical Divinity School still attract the most number of Ivy League (undergraduate) educated Korean-American youths. Even those who studied at Harvard and Yale as undergraduates opt out of going to Harvard Divinity School and Yale Divinity School because they have a strong stigma and prejudice against these seminaries. Korean-American Christian undergraduates at Harvard and Yale consider Harvard Divinity School and Yale Divinity School as instruments of the devil, literally. If one does not believe this, one can go to a Campus Crusade for Christ meeting and ask one of the Korean-American members.

But this hostility against Harvard Divinity School and Yale Divinity School is not abnormal in the American evangelical Christian context. In a country where major Christian leaders – such as Rev. Billy Graham, Rev. Jerry Fawell, and Rev. Pat Robertson – all harbor deep hostility against Harvard Divinity School and Yale Divinity School, it is not surprising to find Korean-American counterparts sharing in their animosity. An average Southern Baptist will hold out a cross to ward off evil at the very mention of Harvard Divinity School and Yale Divinity School. Certainly, getting educated in theology at these seminaries will render the individual practically unemployable in over 80 percent of American churches, which tend toward evangelicalism. Korean undergraduates at Harvard and Yale are merely reflecting the American evangelical sentiment. The difference is that not many of white American evangelicals go to Harvard and Yale to pursue their undergraduate studies. Many evangelical Christians who can get into Harvard and Yale opt to go to a Christian college to learn more about God, to find Christian friends for life, and to find a marriage partner to form a Christian family with. Because the value system of white evangelical Christians is not driven by materialism, the elitism of Harvard and Yale has historically failed to pull conservative white evangelical Christians. But Korean-American Christianity is different. Because Koreans are fundamentally Confucian in outlook, they subscribe to a strong emphasis on elite education, which is a central value of Confucianism next to the Confucian emphasis on human relationships. Thus, whereas white evangelical Christians do not even apply to the Ivy League, places like Harvard and Yale are filled with Korean conservative evangelical Christians who value elite education.

Most liberal and atheist white individuals will not understand the reality of the conservative evangelical Christian world because they will never be exposed to it. But there is an active system of Christian high schools and Christian colleges throughout the United States of America. And many evangelical Christians opt not to go to college at all and start work right away. In fact, less than 35 per cent of all Americans have a college degree or intend to get a college degree. But because in the microcosm of Harvard and Yale Korean evangelical students are highly visible, many liberal, non-Christian whites assume that the Korean dislike of Harvard Divinity School and Yale Divinity School is an aberration particular to Korean Christians, whereas it is fairly normative among white American evangelicals. Just go ask Rev. John Hagee and Rev. John MacArthur what they think about Yale Divinity School. One will notice a flash of hatred come across their face before they answer the question. Hatred for Harvard Divinity School and Yale Divinity School is a driving force behind the formation of conservative evangelical colleges and seminaries like Masters Seminary. One has to be in the conservative evangelical community to understand the aggressive hostility that white American Christians feel toward Harvard Divinity School, Yale Divinity School, and the University of Chicago Divinity School. Since evangelical Christians are the majority of Americans, we are talking about the majority of Americans feeling this way about these seminaries.

Korean-Americans, even the most educated, identify solidly with conservative evangelical Christian faith. Most of them are functionally Fundamentalist Christians – prohibiting drinking, smoking, dancing, and gambling. The conservatism of the American evangelical faith jived well with conservative Korean social mores. Thus, in the collective Korean-American consciousness, the Christian faith is equated with conservative evangelical Christian faith. Conservative evangelical Christian faith is expected by church goers, so even if the clergy wants to be liberal, he will certainly risk losing his job to go against the character of the Korean-American Christianity, which tends toward Fundamentalist Christianity.

Korean-American youths who consciously remain Christians tend to be far more conservative evangelical Christians than their parents. This is an important reality in the Korean-American community that cannot be ignored. This is true of Korean-American youth regardless of whether they go to a Christian school or a public school. This is the case regardless of whether a Korean-American goes to a Christian college or Harvard or Stanford. This identity is so pervasive that it can be said to be characteristic of the Korean-American community. Korean-American youth culture is dominated by conservative evangelical Christian values. Of course, there are exceptions, but the sporadic exceptions prove the rule.

Not everyone will understand what conservative evangelical Christian faith is, so I will explain it for the benefit of readers who are outside of this reality. The reason why conservative evangelical Christian faith is so inaccessible in the American public realm, particularly in the academic realm, can be attributed to two forces. First of all, American mass media tends to be aggressively anti-Christian, particularly against the evangelical Christian kind. There is a reason why both Ronald Reagan and George W. Bush share hostile sentiments against the media. Both of them have pointed to the anti-Christian conspiracy of the American media. Because American media is so aggressively anti-Christian, it is not surprising that there is an aggressive ignorance about the conservative evangelical Christian faith. Despite the fact that the majority of Americans subscribe to conservative evangelical Christian faith, it is a reality that is unknown outside of those who practice it on a daily basis.

There is another reason why conservative evangelical Christian faith is largely missing in public discourse and academic discussions. Besides ignorance based on anti-Christian agenda, there is a general trend toward privacy in regards to one's Christian faith. Thus, even if one's co-worker at a secular workplace is a flaming conservative evangelical Christian, his co-workers may not know. In fact, it is possible for two co-workers to be conservative evangelical Christians, but they may not know this fact. They will be known as Christians but the nature of their Christian faith will not be discussed typically. This is due to the influence of emphasis on the individual relationship to Christ Jesus. Because American Protestants kept emphasizing a personal relationship to Christ, it came to be understood as a private relationship to Christ. Thus, many devout conservative evangelical Christians will keep their Christian faith personal or private. Thus, although the United States has a majority evangelical Christian population, one would not think so because the discourse is missing in the public sphere. This does not mean that conservative evangelical Christian faith is unimportant or irrelevant. In fact, most conservative evangelical Christians will say that it is the most important thing in their life. Most evangelical Christians will be willing to take up arms and start a civil war if they felt that the US government was too far against Christian to be redeemable. The Christian faith is the most important factor in the lives of the majority of Americans, although it remains "private" or "personal" by in large. Just because public discourse is missing does not mean that it is not important (or absent in private group settings). It can be likened to oxygen. One cannot see oxygen. One cannot feel oxygen. And no one even talks about oxygen in normal conversations. But oxygen is important. Without oxygen, one will die. Christian faith is like that and most conservative evangelical Christians will choose death over life for the sake of their conservative Christian faith.

What are the key characteristics of the conservative evangelical Christian faith? They can be grouped under the categories of the Kingdom of Christ, Eternal Life, the Word of God, and Christian Holy Living. First, let us discuss the key characteristic of the Kingdom of Christ. All conservative evangelical Christians will say that they are citizens of the Kingdom of Christ. This is a given; it is assumed and understood to be fact and never questioned in the conservative evangelical Christian community. The Kingdom of Christ is seen as being in Heaven but manifested on earth through Christian believers and the gathering of Christians in the context of the Christian church. For the conservative evangelical Christian, the Kingdom of Christ in Heaven and its manifestation on earth is not equated. This relates to the distinction between the visible church and the invisible church laid out by St. Augustine. It is possible for 90 per cent of "Christians" to go to hell or lose their eternal security for salvation. Church attendance does not guarantee salvation – neither the sacraments of baptism nor the Lord's Supper. Being a member of the Kingdom of Christ is by faith, and faith is the gift of God. Thus, being members of the Kingdom of Christ is seen as conditional on God's choice.

One of the central tenets associated with the idea of the Kingdom of Christ is the key concept that the Christian owes allegiance to Christ the King of kings and the LORD of lords. Thus, conservative evangelical Christians talk about the LORDship of Christ and the need to actively acknowledge the LORDship of Christ. Of course, this is a political statement. To have Christ as King and LORD means that no earthly power can have authority over Christ and the rules of Christ as outlined in the Bible. Thus, when Fundamentalist Christians went around bombing abortion clinics and killing doctors who performed abortions, hardly any Christian church openly condemned them. The fact is, most conservative evangelical Christians sympathize with their actions to uphold the law of the Kingdom of Christ. Because Christian allegiance is to the Kingdom of Christ, breaking earthly secular laws to uphold the laws of Christ the King is fundamentally assumed to be acceptable by most conservative evangelical Christians, regardless of what academic theologians say about the issue from their armchairs and Ivy towers.

Citizenship in the Kingdom of Christ is understood by most normal, everyday Christians to be a political statement. And when push comes to shove, most conservative evangelical Christians will have no problem carrying out a revolution or civil war to uphold the Kingdom of Christ over secular powers. This concept is fundamentally built into the system. Christ is the head of the Kingdom of Christ in Heaven, but it has its earthly manifestation on earth, including the political and social realms. When Christians pray, "Thy will be done on earth as it is in Heaven," they recognize implicitly their duty to the Kingdom of Christ in the political and earthly realms. "For Thine is the Kindgom, and the Power, and the Glory" is not referring to some future event but the present. Most Christians will recognize their pledge of allegiance to the Kingdom of Christ as they pray the Lord's Prayer.

Because the earthly church is seen as the visible church that does not always accurately reflect the wishes of the Kingdom of Christ in Heaven, many conservative evangelical Christians do not go to church. Just because they do not go to church does not mean that they are not loyal to Christ and the Kingdom of Christ. In fact, conservative evangelical Christians in the United States who do not go to church are often more aggressively Fundamentalist Christians with more radical ideas than those who go to church. An estimated 40 million conservative evangelical Christians do not go to church on a regular basis. Many of them turn to Pat Robertson's Christian TV program or hear sermons of Jerry Fawell and other Fundamentalist Christian clergy on radio or TV. They tend to be far more fundamentalist than some 100 million conservative evangelical Christians who go to church every Sunday.[74] Even the 100 million conservative evangelical Christians who go to church regularly will say that their allegiance is with Christ the King and not with their earthly church or even with their pastor. American Protestantism is all about the Kingdom of Christ and citizenship in the Kingdom of Christ. This emphasis is shared regardless of denomination and geographical locality within the United States.

The fact is that the Reformation emphasized the fallacy of the earthly church as a religious institution. Because the pope has been called the anti-Christ for so long in the Protestant tradition, there is a fundamental distrust of the clergy and the earthly institution of the church. Most Protestants view the preaching of their pastor with deep suspicion. In fact, the Reformation encouraged church goers to question their pastors and distrust their preaching. They were exhorted to compare the preaching with the Word of God, the Holy Bible. If the Bible taught something clearly and their pastor condemned the practice demanded in the Bible, then the Protestant tradition taught that they should put the authority of the Bible over the authority of a human being who went against the Bible, including their pastor.

Thus, it is understood that the Kingdom of Christ as manifested on earth through Christian associations and churches can be fallible and the pastor can turn out to be a traitor to the Kingdom of Christ. Deep suspicion of the leadership of the earthly church has existed since Day 1 of the Reformation and persists strongly even this day. Thus, Kingdom of Christ is seen as being in Heaven, invisible, and spiritual. Its manifestation is in the form of the visible church, the body of believers on earth. Protestant Christians do not see their membership in the church as a guarantee of salvation or

---

[74] Korean-American Christianity, although similar to Fundamentalist American (white) Christianity, is different in this aspect. Korean-Americans do not worship via TV or radio. Perhaps because of their ethnic ties to the Korean-American church, Korean-Americans attend church regularly. Generally, over 80% of Korean-American church members will go to the church at least once a week (Lee, *Impact of Ethnic Identity*, p. 61).

ensuring eternal life. Only true citizenship in the Kingdom of Heaven will guarantee that.

This leads into the discussion of Eternal Life, which is another of the key values of the conservative evangelical Christian faith. Protestant Christians have always said that salvation is not in the church but it is in Christ. The church cannot grant salvation or give guarantees for eternal life. Only Christ can give eternal life, and only Christ can guarantee eternal salvation after physical death. Because Protestant Reformers destroyed any right that the Christian clergy had to offer salvation or guarantee eternal life, Protestant Christians do not look to the earthly church for their salvation. This explains why so many evangelical Christians refuse to join an earthly church and prefer to worship Christ in their homes via the TV. It has provided opportunities for many TV evangelists to thrive. These evangelical Christians give their tithes and offering faithfully to the ministry of the TV evangelists. At one time, Rev. Jimmy Swagger's ministry was thought to be worth far more than 100 million dollars. Conservative evangelical Christians typically do not see the difference between going to church and watching a TV evangelist preach on the TV. The emphasis is on the Word of God, not on human gathering, in the conservative evangelical Christian faith.

Conservative evangelical Christians believe that eternal life is only possible through belief that Jesus Christ is God and the only Savior of the world. Thus, the church is incidental to eternal salvation. The only value of the church for a typical conservative evangelical Christian is in the fact that the Word of God can be preached faithfully there so that faith can grow from the hearing of the Word of God. But this can be accomplished just as well by hearing preachers on radio. The Word of God is seen as the power of God. The church is seen as a media center to make this possible, like a TV station or a radio station. And conservative evangelical Christians believe that Christians can become "lapsed" or "fall away" and lose their eternal life. Some conservative evangelical Christians pushing "eternal security" will argue that you cannot lose your salvation if you are truly saved, but they will agree that someone who has "fallen away" was never truly saved in the first place. This amounts to the same thing. A person who was recognized to be a true born-again believer is no longer truly born again – whether he has lost the salvation or whether he was never saved in the first place is merely semantics. Conservative Christians believe that a betrayal of the Kingdom of Christ and a rejection of the duties as a Christian to accept the LORDship of Christ will result in a state where one will not experience eternal life. Thus, for conservative evangelical Christians, salvation is through faith in Jesus Christ, but one can never be sure of one's eternal life until one stands before the judgment seat of God because one can "fall away" or was "not truly saved in the first place." The conviction of salvation one had at age 17 was misguided – one had fooled herself but one were not really saved in the first place. For conservative evangelical Christians, eternal life can be lost, in effect.

And faith in Christ which brings eternal life comes as the result of the Word of God. Thus, the Word of God is another central value in the conservative evangelical Christian faith. There is a reason why many Southern Baptist missionaries risked their lives to smuggle in Bibles behind the Iron Curtain during the days of the Cold War. They believed that salvation could not come apart from the Word of God. This goes back to the Reformation emphasis of *sola scriptura*. The Reformers emphasized that there is no salvation in the earthly church. Justification was by faith only. Thus, the Holy Bible was emphasized as the only standard to measure anything in life. Because church members were encouraged to criticize the teachings of the church based on the Word of God, literacy was highly emphasized in Protestant areas. The emphasis on the Word of God, however, decentralized the church, so that many Christian denominations formed. Most Protestants have no problems changing denominations. In fact, conservative evangelical faith is not confined to a particular denomination. In every denomination in the United States, one will find conservative evangelicals.

It is natural that those who emphasize the Word of God will emphasize Holy Living. Both the Old Testament and the New Testament emphasize holy living. In fact, the New Testament states that a Christian cannot go to heaven with certain sins. Thus, even if one is born again, he cannot go to Heaven if he is perpetually living in sin. The New Testament emphasis that one who perpetually commits sin cannot enter Heaven has spurred many holiness movements and revivals in America. For instance, during the Great Awakening, Rev. Jonathan Edwards (the first president of what is now Princeton University) threatened his baptized church members (they were all baptized as infants), that they were risking Hell. The sermon was entitled, "Sinners in the Hands of an Angry God." The fact that Jonathan Edwards preached a sermon threatening hell to a room full of professing born-again Christians must be emphasized. Jonathan Edwards implicitly believed that a Christian can lose his salvation (which is explained sometimes as "you were never saved in the first place").

Because conservative evangelical Christians believe that one can lose her salvation, Holy Living became a key value in the conservative evangelical Christian mind. The majority of the American population are conservative evangelical Christians who believe that Holy Living is essential for entrance into Heaven. That is why there is an emphasis in trying to live a holy life and repentance when one fails. And true repentance is defined in the conservative evangelical Christian circles as "turning away from sin to God." One cannot be seen as truly repentant if one continues in her sin. Thus, if a person commits adultery, but repents, theoretically her sin is forgiven. But if she goes and commits adultery again the next week and the week after that, conservative evangelical Christians will assume that her repentance is not genuine and she is not a true believer. Conservative evangelical Christians in the United States emphasize that "ye shall know them by their fruit," which means that the sign of being a true Christian is in holy living. Those who do not live a holy life cannot be a true Christian by definition in the minds of conservative evangelical Christians.

Those Christians who say that they were born again will lose their salvation (or was not saved in the first place), if they live a life of sin. They will go to eternal damnation in Hell. This is the fundamental value of conservative evangelical Christianity.

By in large Korean-American Christianity subscribes to this emphasis of conservative evangelical Christians of America, who comprise the majority of the American population.[75] In a sense, therefore, Korean-American Christianity can be seen as an integral part of the conservative evangelical Christianity of America. The problem is that socially Korean-American Christians and white conservative evangelical Christians do not mix. Furthermore, there is the color line that divides Korean evangelical Christians from white evangelical Christians. But it the similarity in applied theology and Christian outlook cannot be denied.

Understanding the nature of Korean-American Christianity in America, most of which tends to be conservative evangelical Christian, can help in better understanding of Korean-American individuals and the Korean-American community. Because Korean-Americans have historically socialized in the Korean-American church context, much of the conservative evangelical Christian outlook has become the outlook of many Korean-Americans. To a large extent, the conservative evangelical *weltanschauung* plays in integral and central role as Korean-Americans endorse it or react against it (as is the case with some younger Korean-Americans).

---

[75] Chae-Kun Yu, "The Correlates of Cultural Assimilation of Korean Immigrants in the United States," *The Korean Diaspora: Historical and Sociological Studies of Korean Immigrants and Assimilation in North America*, ed. Hyung-Chan Kim (Santa Barbara: ABC-Clio, Inc., 1977, pp. 167-176), p. 173.

Heerak Christian Kim

Chapter 4:
"Understanding the Korean-American Family"

It would be fair to say that it is impossible to understand the Korean-American individual identity and the Korean-American corporate identity without understanding the nature of the Korean-American family. For Korean-Americans, the Korean-American family is the most important social institution.[76] This is true for Korean-Americans who were born in the United States and attend Princeton University as much as it is for Koreans who just immigrated from South Korea to live permanently in the United States. The family is the most important social unit in the Korean collective consciousness because its value has been aggressively pushed by the Confucian kingdom of the Yi Dynasty, which existed for 800 years in Korea, up to the beginning of the Japanese Occupation of Korea (1910-1945). Even before the Yi Dynasty, which made Confucianism the official philosophy of the Yi Dynasty, Koreans followed Confucian dictates regarding the family. Thus, Confucian influence on Koreans extend over 2000 years.

Confucianism is often mistakenly referred to as a religion. This is highly inaccurate way of perceiving Confucianism. Confucianism is more like a philosophy or a worldview. Just as Helle-

---

[76] Kwang Chung Kim and Won Moo Hurh, "The Extended Conjugal Family: Family-Kinship System of Korean Immigrants in the United States," *The Korean-American Community: Present and Future*, eds. Tae-Hwan Kwak and Seong Hyong Lee (Seoul: Kyungnam University Press, 1991, pp. 115-133), p. 117.

nistic philosophy impacted Judaism as evident in the writings of Philo of Alexandria, Confucianism impacted Buddhism, which is an Asian religion. Just because Philo of Alexandria embraced Hellenistic philosophy and used it actively to explain Judaism did not mean that he had changed religions. Philo of Alexandria was religiously Jewish. He perceived himself that way and others perceived him that way. Most importantly, Jewish religious authorities perceived Philo of Alexandria as being within Judaism and his ideas as compatible with Jewish religious ideas. Hellenistic philosophy is a philosophical system that can be employed to explain an existing religious tradition.

In the same way, Confucianism is a philosophical system. And as a philosophical system, it impacted people holding to Buddhism. There is sometimes confusion because Buddhist philosophers had a political battle with Confucian philosophers in the context of the Korean society. Even Korean monarchs misunderstood the nature of the conflict. But this is not surprising. It can be compared with the conflict in the Late Second Temple period among elite priestly families. There were high priests aggressively pushing Hellenistic philosophy in the Jerusalem Temple. They saw themselves as faithful to Judaism as long as they applied Hellenistic philosophy and did not impede Jewish religious practices. Hellenistic philosophy was a philosophy and not a religion.

This raises the question. What is a religion and what is a philosophy? Simply put, religion can be seen as involving religious rituals, which the members of the religion are expected to participate in. Although rituals may be subsumed under religious belief or faith system, all religions have rituals that are expected to be practiced. In contrast, philosophy is an idea. The idea can impose certain actions on the individual or the group but they are not identified as religious rituals. Rather, actions which philosophy solicits involves individual and corporate behaviors that are detached from distinctively religious rituals. In contrast, religions require rituals that are seen as separated from the secular realm.

This is what Mercea Eliade calls the distinction between the sacred and the profane. This is missing in a philosophy.

Furthermore, religions require actions done for God or a deity. In contrast, philosophy may require an action, but that action is not done for a divine being or divine presence. In this regard, the relationship of Hellenistic philosophy to Judaism makes sense. Judaism of the Late Second Temple period required ritualistic observance that was consciously done for God and God's requirement on the Jews. Jews understood their actions to be such. In contrast, Hellenistic philosophy made no religious demands on Jews. Jews can embrace Hellenistic philosophy and follow its emphasis – for example, its emphasis about true friendship as a virtue – but this did not involve any type of consciousness in regards to fulfilling some religious duty to God or a divine being.

In the same way, Confucianism is a philosophy and not a religion. Whereas one can find Buddhist temples, one cannot find Confucian places of worship or Confucian religious centers meant to be used for religious rituals. The fact is that Confucianism was formed as a philosophy and it existed as a philosophy, and not as a religion. Like Hellenism vis-à-vis Judaism, there were Buddhists who resisted Confucian philosophical influences on Buddhism. Like the Essenes who ran off into the desert to lead a pure Jewish remnant in protest of rampant Hellenistic influence on Judaism in the Jerusalem Temple, there were Buddhists who resisted Confucian influences on Buddhism aggressively. However, just because Jewish religious authorities resisted Hellenistic influences does not make Hellenistic philosophy a religion. In the same way, just because there were at times hostile and aggressive resistance to the influence of Confucian philosophy on Buddhism does not mean that Confucian philosophy is a religion.

The fact is that Hellenistic philosophy was pervasive in the Late Second Temple period. Even the reformist Jews of the time were deeply impacted by Hellenistic philosophy. It is no accident that the greatest apologists for the Jewish religion, Philo of Alexandria, was heavily influenced by Hellenistic philosophy and utilized Hellenistic philosophy consciously to defend the value of Judaism. Many scholars of Rabbinic Judaism point out that there are Hellenistic philosophical influences evident in the Talmud, the primary Jewish religious text for Rabbinic Judaism. Hellenistic philosophical influence was pervasive in the Late Second Temple period. In the same way, Confucian influences were pervasive in Korea for over a thousand years.

In fact, the Confucian influence was so great that political institutions and social structures were often ordered according to the Confucian philosophical system. China, which also was heavily influenced by Confucianism, arranged its international policy based on Confucian philosophy and consciously modified Confucian philosophy to order its relations with its neighboring countries. Thus, according to Confucian emphasis on the family, China started to order the nations around it in terms of familial relationship. Thus, Korea became the little brother and was expected to fulfil the obligations expected of a little brother to a big brother. Because all Koreans were aware of Confucian philosophy and even unconsciously operated according to Confucian dictates in their family relationships, it was not difficult for Korea to know instinctively what was expected by China of Korea when it was designated as a "little brother" nation. And history shows that Korea faithfully fulfilled the Confucian value of the relationship of the little brother to his big brother in its international relationship to China.

For non-Koreans and for Korean-Americans not very familiar with the Korean society in South Korea, it is important to point out social institutions that clearly serve as evidence of Confucian influence. First of all, there is the "Sunbae System." The Sunbae System is pervasive throughout Korea – both in North Korea and in South Korea. It is a product of Korean history for centuries. The Sunbae System can be explained in terms of "little brother – big brother relationship."[77] And the requirements of this system follow Confucian dictates regarding the relationship between the big brother and the little brother in a family.

The little brother must show respect and give honor proactively to the big brother. And the little brother must obey the command of the big brother. That is the duty of the little brother within the Confucian system. In the Korean society, the big brother can command the little brother not to marry the woman he loves and in theory he has to comply. The failure to comply will have dire consequences within the Confucian system. Thus, when someone in Korea wants to marry a girl, he must not only get the permission of his parents, but his big brother as well. The importance of this point is born in the fact that after a Korean wedding ceremony, the newly married Korean couple must give an honorific greeting to their parents and all who are older than they within their extended family structure, including the big brother. The way the married couple give the honorific greeting is that they stand before the one receiving the honorific greeting and then they prostrate themselves completely to the ground in the way that servants prostrate themselves before Oriental monarchs. This is an influence from Confucianism and it emphasizes the little brother's recognition of the sovereignty of the big brother and all who are older than him. It is a symbolic promise that he and his wife will obey whatever they will command them to obey in marriage.

The importance of the big brother – little brother relationship cannot be stressed enough in the Korean family. Traditionally, Korean little brothers are not even allowed to talk to the big brother as an equal. Fundamentally, by Confucian system, the little brother is inferior by the order of Heaven. The fact that he was born after the big brother is the evidence that it goes against Nature for the little brother to usurp his big brother's cosmological place in the world. The rule for little brother still operates in South Ko-

---

[77] Andrew Sung Park, *Racial Conflict and Healing: An Asian-American Theological Perspective* (Maryknoll: Orbis Books, 1996), p. 121.

rea and North Korea, and its violation will bring down on his head great dishonor. This dishonor can result in social ostracization, being fired from his job, and even arrest, as Korean laws reflect a Confucian worldview regarding how the world should be ordered.

To give an example of the pervasive nature of this Confucian philosophy, I would point to the obligation of the wife of the little brother. The wife of the little brother under Confucianism must honor the big brother. Thus, even if she is socially elite and is the queen of South Korea, she must cowtow to the older brother and his wife, who may be barely screeching by in poverty. They must bow down in showing honor, and they must not address them as equals. The Korean language clearly distinguishes between equals and superiors. The wife of the younger brother must use the honorific language with the big brother and his wife even if they are of higher "social status" according to the West. Furthermore, just as the little brother is expected to obey the big brother, the wife of the little brother must obey the command of the big brother and the wife of the big brother. These are strong requirements in the Confucian system. The wife refusing to abide by the Confucian system will bring about condemnation of the Korean community and her virtue and character will be seriously questioned. Depending on the gravity of the disobedience, she can be ostracized and all her social honors taken away instantaneously. All her life's work to gain respect and honor will mean nothing if she proactively opposes the Confucian requirements for the little brother and his wife to the big brother and the wife of the big brother.

And this is the obligation of the big brother to the little brother. The big brother is to give wise advice to the little brother so he will not go astray or make a big mistake in life. A big brother who does not give advice is seen to be violating his obligations to Confucian requirements placed on the big brother. If the little brother refuses to listen to big brother's good advice, the big brother has the right within the Confucian system to beat up his little brother physically and knock sense into him. The Korean police will not arrest a big brother beating up the little brother almost to the point of death because the Korean law protects the right of the big brother to defend the family honor and "counsel" the little brother according to the Confucian system, which is the philosophical underpinning for Korean laws. Of course, there is a checks-and-balances system built into Confucianism. The big brother is not to make onerous demands on the little brother or require him to do unreasonable things. The duties of the big brother to little brother is understood in the Korean society as Confucian philosophy has been applied and practiced within the context of the Korean family for centuries. It is ingrained in the culture, collective memory, and individual psyche.

The above applies to an actual family. However, just as China applied the Confucian philosophy of the relationship between the little brother and the big brother to its international relations and political institutions, Koreans applied this Confucian philosophy to relationships of non-blood tied individuals in the Korean society. Thus, the "Sunbae System" was developed. This system is known to have existed as long as Confucianism existed in Korea. Certainly, the Korean society today functions along the Sunbae System at every level and in every sphere.

What is the Sunbae System? It is the system where the younger member of an organization must relate to the older member of an organization in terms of the little brother – big brother relationship guiding Korean families in applied Confucian philosophy. Thus, a Korean who is one year ahead of another Korean in elementary school is his Sunbae, or "fictive older brother." The younger Korean (called "Hoobae" in the Korean language) is required to show respect and honor to his Sunbae. And this requirement is for life. Thus, even after the Sunbae and the Hoobae graduate from elementary school and they go on to different junior high schools, the Sunbae System is in effect. Even if they go completely separate ways after elementary school and meet back after 80 years, the Sunbae System and its requirements apply the moment they see each other. The system is so important that there are reunions of elementary school graduates. The elementary school reunions, which occur throughout one's life until one dies, generally is meant to reinforce the Sunbae System.

Even in the United States, the Sunbae System applies. Thus, if a Korean in Los Angeles runs into his elementary school Sunbae, he must show him honor and respect due to that relationship under the Confucian system. The failure to abide by the Confucian system will bring down dishonor in the context of the Los Angeles Korean community. The violator of the Sunbae System can find himself losing close friends who expect him to abide by the Confucian system, experience ostracization in the Korean community in Los Angeles, and see loss of Korean customers who will not shop at his store on principle because they value the Confucian system. Thus, a Korean who refuses to show honor and respect to his elementary school Sunbae whom he has not seen in 30 years can result in his complete disenfranchisement from the Korean community in Los Angeles and even loss of his job or economic status in the Korean society.

This is why the Hoobae ("the fictive little brother in the Korean fictive kinship system") who has an issue with the Sunbae will avoid him and will become invisible. The Sunbae System requires his active respect and show of honor to Sunbae, no matter how he may personally feel about him, when he is in his conscious presence. The violation of the Sunbae System in the conscious realm will result in his complete disenfranchisement in the Korean community. This is why Sunbae can yell at the Hoobae and the Hoobae cannot talk back. The most aggressive form of protest can be departing the presence of the Sunbae.

To illustrate this, I will share a story of the Sunbae System at work at my father's church. There was an elder in the church. In the Presbyterian church system, an elder is the highest ruling authority in the church. It is the place of greatest honor. He happened to be an elementary Hoobae ("fictive little brother") to a deacon in the church. The position of the deacon is "lower" in the Presbyterian hierarchy. In the church context, the deacon showed the church elder, his Hoobae, respect because of the position he held in the church. And the church elder always showed respect to the church deacon far more than he did to anybody else, including the pastor, because he was his Sunbae. One time the elder opposed the policy of the senior pastor of the church and gave the senior pastor a hard time. He said on matter of his principles. The Sunbae, the deacon in the church who held an "inferior" position in the church, happened to like the pastor. So, the deacon went over to the house of the elder and told him to stop opposing the pastor. The elder refused to listen, and the deacon beat him up physically. The elder could not throw a single punch because beating up a Sunbae in the conscious realm means social suicide in Korea. All the Sunbae has to do is go around and recall the Sunbae System actively within the Korean community and the Hoobae will have no place to stand within the Korean context.

    The wife of the elder stood by watching her husband get beat up and did nothing. She is not supposed to protest in the Korean system. The Sunbae has the right to beat up a Hoobae in cases of extreme violation of the Sunbae System. It is seen as normal. The following Sunday, the elder came with bruises and a black eye. Everyone in the church knew what happened because the wife of the Sunbae told everyone in the Korean community. The Hoobae was given credit because he did not fight the Sunbae but let him beat him up. Thus, the elder was allowed to keep his social standing in the Korean community. Not a single person in the church condemned the beating because they implicitly understood the right of the Sunbae to beat up the Hoobae within the understood guidelines of the Sunbae System. The Sunbae System is for life. The Sunbae of the elementary school is Sunbae for life, and the Hoobae has to show respect and honor throughout his life. Because the Sunbae System is for life, it does not matter what economic wealth one obtains or social status one achieves or an office one holds, he is bound by the Sunbae System for life. Thus, in the context of the church, the deacon is "inferior" to the elder, but under the Sunbae System the elder will be inferior to the deacon for life. The Sunbae System trumps any other social system in Korea.

Thus, even the Korean President must respect his Sunbae, and if his Sunbae wants to beat him up because of the violation of the Sunbae System, he must take the beating. The Korean President opposing the Sunbae System is tantamount to his political, social and personal suicide. His body guards will refuse to protect him in times of trouble if he violates the Sunbae System. It is implicitly understood to be the most important social relationship system operating in Korea.

Thus, elementary reunions still go on in the USA among Koreans. And there are reunions for high schools and colleges. Generally, the Sunbae system that operates until college are seen to be the most strong Sunbae System and trumps any other kind of Sunbae System in the future. Thus, an elementary school Sunbae is a Sunbae for life even if he is inferior to his Hoobae in the church for 20 years. He can at any point recall the Sunbae System and with a legitimate recall, the church elder who is his elementary school Hoobae has to comply to the legitimate demands. Generally, in the Confucian philosophy, the earlier Sunbae system trumps the later Hoobae system. Thus, if an elementary school Sunbae is held back a year in high school because he flunks and graduates later than his Hoobae from high school, his position as Sunbae is not lost. He is Sunbae for life and that cannot be changed, whether his elementary school Hoobae becomes a "superior" in the church 30 years later or if his Hoobae graduates earlier from high school and advances faster in college than he. No social advancement or economic wealth takes away the Sunbae right of the elementary Sunbae. Confucianism is not like Christianity or even like Judaism. You cannot sell your birthright – that is impossible in Confucianism. Even if you sell your birthright, you retain your birthright. Your birthright is seen as a part of the Ordered Universe and cannot be changed. In the same way, a Sunbae cannot lose his Sunbae status once it is established in elementary school merely by the fact that they have attended the same elementary school. Nature has placed you in that relationship and you are bound by Heaven to respect the Sunbae System.

The Sunbae System is an integral part of the Korean society. It is the central functioning system within the Korean-American society, particularly in the context of the Korean-American church, which seeks to preserve the Korean culture. Every clergy in the Korean-American church operates under the guideline of the Sunbae System. When the system is recalled, they must come in line. Failure to come in line under the Sunbae System will result in the loss of personal status and honor and even the loss of job and friends. Because the whole Korean society is ordered according to the Sunbae System, everyone has something to lose from its dilution. Thus, even if a person hates someone, he will uphold his rights as a Sunbae. Violating the Sunbae System will send the Korean society into chaos. More importantly on a personal level, a person who disrespects the rights of a Sunbae, even if he is his enemy, will lose his own rights according to the Confucian ordering of the world, to receive respect from his Hoobae. Because Confucian philosophy perceives violation of the Sunbae System as the violation of the Created Order, anyone violating the Sunbae System is seen as the violator of the Created Order. Thus, he forfeits his right to make claims on the Sunbae System. Even his own Hoobae who may share in the hatred of his Sunbae for the guy X will recognize the obligation of his Sunbae to uphold the Sunbae System for the guy X. The Created Order is at stake. Every Korean knows the implication of the Sunbae System for Korean identity and for Korean communities around the world.

Interestingly enough, all Korean-Americans operate from the Sunbae System or try to operate from the Sunbae System if they perceive themselves to be Korean in any way. This is visible and noticeable in the context of the Korean-American church. Teenagers who are born in America try to understand the Sunbae System and try to operate within the context of that perception. Not all Korean-Americans born in America understand the Sunbae System fully, but most understand the main gist of the system. Thus, when one goes to Harvard or UCLA, one sees that Korean-Americans born in the USA recognize the Sunbae System as operating and they try to abide by it. Most Korean-Americans will come into line if the Sunbae System is consciously recalled and its principles emphasized. To be Korean means to respect the Sunbae System. Any Korean who does not respect the Sunbae System is deemed not to be Korean or an evil Korean. Korean identity is prefigured along Confucian lines. This Confucian philosophy is just as important for Christians as for non-Christians. In fact, Christians uphold the Confucian philosophical system much more aggressively than non-Christians because the Korean-American church is the primary medium of Korean culture in the United States. That is why weddings done in the Korean-American church will be followed by the traditional Korean cowtowing to the elders in the family including the big brother. Most Koreans instinctively assume the Confucian system as righteous and no church will pro-actively oppose the Confucian system regulating the Korean marriage or any other Korean cultural practice. One of the reasons why Koreans aggressively oppose their sons marrying white women is because they believe that the white woman will not fulfil the Confucian obligation required of the wife to the mother-in-law. There are many requirements.

To this date, no Korean Christian ever complained about Confucian requirements proactively and in print, although some have complained about Buddhist practices of ancestor worship. Whereas worshipping dead ancestors in Buddhist traditions are seen as idolatrous, showing respect to living human beings is not. Confucianism is assumed to be compatible with Christianity by all Korean Christians and the active practice of Korean-American churches and Korean-Americans support this.

If fictive little brother – big brother relationship in the Sunbae System is this important, you can imagine how important the real little brother – big brother relationship is. The little brother in a family who violates his obligations to the big brother required under the Confucian system suffers social setback within the Korean context. Still, the majority of Koreans call their older brother "hyung." In the Korean culture, one is not allowed to say the name of the big brother, so one calls the big brother "hyung," meaning "older brother." If you go to churches today, you can see many Korean-Americans who are born in the USA abiding by this Korean system. Even those Banana Koreans who refuse to call their older brother "hyung" will do so if told to by other Korean-Americans. They understand what is expected in the Korean culture and will comply when they are called on to do so by other members of the Korean-American community.

The Korean-American family, by in large, operates from the Confucian vantage point.[78] This is true of the relationship between the little brother and the big brother. And this is true of the relationship between parents and children. How does the Korean-American family reflect the Confucian value of the relationship between parents and children?

In Confucianism, the relationship between parents and the children are seen as a relationship that is ordered by Heaven. It is an essential relationship that is meant to be a part of the Created Order and should reflect the well-functioning of that Created Order. Under Confucian philosophy, parents are obligated to take care of the children and provide the children with the best education possible. These are the primary obligations of the parents. Under the responsibility to take care of the children is the requirement to see to their physical and moral growth. Thus, it is the responsibility of Korean parents to "nag" their children to be good. And this responsibility is for life. Whereas in America, parents are careful about telling their children what to do after a certain age, certainly after the children have reached 18 years old, under Confucian philosophy, Korean parents are obligated to tell what their children should do until they die. Failure to "impart wisdom" is a failure to act according to the Created Order and fulfil their Confucian obligations as parents. Korean parents take their Confucian obligations seriously as many Korean-American youths will testify. When one

---

[78] Kim, "The Protestant Church and the Korean-American Community," p. 197.

asks Korean-American adults, they too will confirm that their parents rigorously fulfil their Confucian obligations.

Besides taking care of the children, Confucian philosophy requires that Korean parents provide their children with the best education possible. There is a reason why there are so many Koreans in the Ivy League and elite universities like Stanford and UCLA. Korean parents take their Confucian obligation very seriously. There is a saying in the Korean-American community that even Koreans who do not know one word of English will know Harvard University. One can go to the remotest village in South Korea and people will know Harvard University. If one asks Korean-American teenagers if their parents ever mentioned Harvard University, nearly 100 per cent will tell her that their parents have bugged them to go to Harvard University ever since they were little children. Korean-American parents feel a Confucian obligation to provide their children with the best possible education in America. One of the ways they do this is by emphasizing that their children study a lot so that they could get into Harvard University to get educated at the best university in America.

Another aspect of providing the children with the best possible education possible involves a financial aspect. Even in this regard, Korean parents will not fail in fulfilling their obligation to Confucian philosophy and the Created Order. Typical middle class white American parents will refuse to take out a second mortgage to pay for a $200,000 Harvard University undergraduate education for their son, so that even if he is accepted at Harvard University, he has to go to a less expensive, inferior university. This will never ever happen with Korean families. Korean parents will not think twice about taking out a second mortgage to pay for a Harvard University education if their son gets into Harvard. If they cannot take out a second mortgage, they will take out a personal loan from the bank to pay for their children's Harvard University education. If they cannot take out a personal loan from the bank to pay for their son's Harvard University education, they will go and borrow money from their friends and acquaintances to pay for their son's $200,000 Harvard University education. Most Koreans will loan money out to parents seeking to fulfil their Confucian obligation as parents. It is expected in the Korean society. If a Korean-American parent refuses to go into $200,000 in debt to send his son to Harvard University, he will be utterly disgraced in the Korean community and all his honors will be taken away. He may even lose his job if his employer is Korean. Confucian obligations of parents are held to be sacred in the Korean community.

Thus, Korean-American parents are expected to sell their house and move into an apartment if their son is accepted at Harvard and the only way to pay for his education is by selling his only home. Not doing this will make the Korean parents bad parents and they will be ostracized in the Korean community. Education is not understood to be a luxury item, but an essential obligation of the Korean parents.[79] This point is nowhere more evident than in the Korean context where Confucian philosophy reigns supreme. There were bright Koreans in rural areas who studied hard and were accepted to Seoul National University, which is the best university in South Korea. They had no money to go to Seoul, the nation's capital, and study at Seoul National University. So, what did the parents of these Korean youth in the rural area do? They sold their family farm, which has been passed down to them for generations and which was the only source of family income and livelihood. If a boy, a son of a farmer, was accepted to Seoul National University, it would be unthinkable for his parents to suggest that he be a farmer like generations of his ancestors and farm the family land. That would rain down utter contempt of all the farmers in his rural area because Confucian philosophy reigns supreme in the most uneducated, rural areas of Korea. They know that their Confucian obligation requires them to provide their children with the best education possible. Thus, the parents will sell the family

---

[79] Kim, "Career Prospects of Korean Immigrants' Children," *The Emerging Generation of Korean-Americans*, eds. Ho-Youn Kwon and Shin Kim (Seoul: Kyong Hee University Press, 1993, pp. 107-123), p. 119.

farm. They will understand that to be their obligation to their Confucian duty as parents. And all of their neighbors will understand that they must do this to fulfil their Confucian obligations.

When the parents fulfil their Confucian obligations and sell their only plot of farming land and the only source of livelihood, neighbors will approve and give honor to the parents. Furthermore, because they have fulfilled their Confucian duty, the neighbors in the rural village will find a way for the parents to survive although they no longer have livelihood or have work. Generally, the people who bought the farmland will allow them to farm the land for a small payment and allow them to stay on in their home as renters. Houses of farmers are generally on the farmland. Confucian obligation trumps any other value in the Korean society. There are many Korean farmers from all corners of the Korean society and there is not a single account of parents failing to meet their Confucian obligation by selling their family farm to pay for their children's college education in the event they are accepted at an expensive university in Seoul.

Korean-Americans are guided by this Confucian philosophical principle, and this Confucian value trumps every ethical and moral value system in the Korean society. Confucianism is the overarching philosophical system that undergirds every social institution in Korea and has been an influential societal guide for 2,000 years in the Korean peninsula. There is not a single Christian in Korea or in America or around the world who is ethnically Korean and sees himself as a Korean, who will not follow Confucian guidelines. If he objected, then he would have to live outside of the Korean community, wherever he is. He will be rejected in the Korean-American church and members of the Korean-American society will ostracize him. Confucian guidelines are the most important of any philosophical system in the Korean communities around the world.

What are the obligations of the children to their parents? In the Confucian philosophical system, children's obligations to their parents are to study hard and achieve the greatest education possible and to take care of their parents in their old age.[80] Because the Confucian system created a relatively fair system where professional advancement was guaranteed through educational achievement, studying hard and achieving academically equalled success. Confucian economic system is not a Calvinist driven capitalist economic system based on supply and demand or is it based on Darwinian influenced survival of the fittest system where unfair policies for competitive edge is tolerated. Confucian system is built on a simple system that equates academic achievement with professional advancement. Thus, it can be seen as a truly meritocratic system devoid of laissez-faire competition to upset meritocratic advancement.

Of course, Korean-Americans find themselves in a capitalist system and in the midst of discrimination against Asians, which is a foreign concept to Asians. Thus, many Korean-American parents cannot understand why their son who received a 3.7 in economics from the University of California at Berkeley will be laid off after 2 years of working in an accounting firm. This would not happen in Korea. The reason that such things occur in the United States of America is that there is a glass ceiling for Asian-Americans. Merely based on the color of their skin, Asian-Americans suffer in white firms and are often overlooked for advancement. When a company wants to restructure and fire some people, the first people to lay off tend to be Asian-Americans. Historic discrimination against Asian-Americans is a historical fact supported by historical evidence, US laws passed in the past against Asians, and social policies on record that clearly prove discrimination against Asian-Americans. But many Korean-Americans are completely ignorant of Asian-American history or of modern American history. Thus, Korean-American parents operate from a pure Confucian system thinking that academic

---

[80] Sunok Shun Pai, "The Changing Role of Korean-Americans," *The Emerging Generation of Korean-Americans*, eds. Ho-Youn Kwon and Shin Kim (Seoul: Kyung Hee University Press, 1993, pp. 215-224), p. 218.

achievement will necessarily lead to professional success. This may be more the case among white Americans who do not have to put up with discrimination against the people of color, but for Asian-Americans who are visibly a people of color, the formula is not that simple. There is rampant discrimination against Asian-Americans in today's America, and there are ample records to prove the reality.

Despite the ignorance about white America's discrimination against Asian-Americans for being a people of color and the general ignorance about modern American history, Korean-American society functions with Confucian guidelines and believes that academic achievement will equal professional success. Although the formula is not as neat as in Korea, to a large extent this formula is the only formula available to Korean-Americans. Although highly achieving Korean-Americans will suffer discrimination and be targeted by white America (whether the whites be Jews, Muslims, or Christians), consciously or unconsciously, what can the Korean-American youth do to ensure their success in the American society? They cannot change the color of their skin to white; they are born a people of color and they will die visibly as a people of color. The color of one's skin cannot be changed. Since this is a constant, the only thing that Korean-Americans have to work with is education. So, in a sense Confucian philosophy is the key to Korean-American survival in the American context. The rule of thumb operating in the United States is that Korean-Americans have to achieve at least three times (3X) the skill of white Americans to secure a position that someone who is white and three times (3X) inferior will secure. Thus, if a Korean-American wants an engineering job at a white American company, he must be 3X as qualified as a white individual to get a job of same pay and same position (especially, over the long-run) as the white American who is 3X less qualified than he. This rule operates for Korean-Americans in every profession in the white American setting.

Most Korean-American youth are faithful to their Confucian obligations to their Korean-American parents. They may not consciously understand that they are fulfilling their obligations when they study very hard, but they are. The Confucian obligation is internalized in the Korean psyche through 1,500 years of Confucian philosophical dominance in Korea. Koreans and Korean-Americans operate from the Confucian reference point without consciously thinking or even aware that they are doing so. In the same manner, most Korean-American youth operate from the Confucian vantage point and study very hard. They are studying hard and fulfilling their Confucian obligations to their Korean parents.

And interestingly enough, Korean-American youth seem to be aware that they have an obligation to take care of their parents when they get old.[81] They may not consciously know that the reason why they feel or think this way is because of their Confucian heritage, but despite their lack of conscious awareness, Korean-American youth operate from a Confucian vantage point. Won H. Chang writes: "Elderly parents are the center of authority in the traditional Korean family and community. Their care is not an option, but a moral responsibility. The family which does not revere its elderly parents actually is rebelling against the unwritten law and order and traditional values of the community."[82] Taking care of parents in their old age is not an American value. How many Americans fully pay for their parents from month to month (housing, food costs, spending money, all other costs) from the moment they retire until they die? Many Korean-American families take on 100 per cent of the parents' financial burden once the parents retire. This is the Confucian way, not the American way. Not a single American church in the United States will tell their church members to bear 100 per cent of their parents' living costs after retire-

---

[81] Kim and Hurh, "The Extended Conjugal Family," p. 122.
[82] Won H. Chang, "Communication and Acculturation," *The Korean Diaspora: Historical and Sociological Studies of Korean Immigration and Assimilation in North America*, ed. Hyung-Chan Kimi (Santa Barbara: ABC-Clio, Inc., 1977, pp. 135-154), p. 146.

ment. American Christianity refuses to acknowledge that it is a Christian thing to take care of the parents in their old age with 100 per cent financial support.

The Korean-American Church stands completely opposed to white American Christianity in this regard. Korean-American churches will preach that the Korean-American youth must bear 100 per cent of the financial burden of their parents after their parents retire until they die. This lesson is born from Confucian philosophy or the Confucian worldview. This philosophical system is incorporated into Christianity, which is a religion, and not a philosophy. For white American Christianity, individualism[83] of the Renaissance period became the philosophy that was incorporated into white American Christianity, and white American Church teaching regarding parents and taking care of the parents in the old age reflects the impact of philosophy of individualism that has impacted white Americans, regardless of religion.

This becomes clear when one compares white Christians with white non-Christians. There is absolutely no difference between white Christian Church teaching about what the children should do with their retired parents and what the white American secular society teaches about what the children should do with their retired parents. The congruence between church teaching and non-Christian white American position underscores the point that it is the philosophy of individualism that operates both in the white Christian sphere and the white secular (or atheist) sphere. With Koreans, the philosophy that operates is Confucianism. Whether a Korean is a Christian or a non-Christian or a Buddhist, Confucianism is the philosophical element and worldview that dictate children's relationship to their parents. Thus, whether a Korean-American is Buddhist, atheist, or Christian, he is expected to give 100 per cent financial support to his Korean-American parents. Confucian philosophy for Koreans is like the philosophy of indi-

---

[83] Park, *Racial Conflict and Healing*, p. 121.

vidualism for white Americans of European descent vis-à-vis their religious commitments.

Most Korean-American youth understand their obligation to take care of their parents. Many mistakenly think that this is a Christian obligation.[84] Obviously, taking care of 100 per cent of their parents' financial needs after retirement is not a Christian obligation. If it were a Christian obligation, then white American churches would teach it, but they do not. White American Christians do not support their parents financially, generally. They are busy looking for inheritance from them. Korean-American Christian children do not expect inheritance from their parents because inheritance system is not an integral element in the Confucian system. Korean children are to support their parents in their old age and parents are expected to have spent all their possessions providing best education possible for their children and helping them set up their professional careers. It is a Confucian value and not a Christian value. But because Korean-American churches teach the Confucian value of the children's obligation to provide 100 per cent for their parents' financial needs after retirement, Korean-American Christian youth assume that it is a Christian teaching. There is absolutely not a single American or a European theologian today who has written a book stating that children should provide for 100 per cent of the financial need of their parents and that is a Christian value. It is not a Christian value or regarded as important in Christianity. It is a Confucian philosophical worldview which Korean-American Christians have adopted into the Christian religion. But in upholding this Confucian value, Korean-American Christians do not have solidarity with white Christians; in fact, they are diametrically opposed to the white Christian emphasis on individualism as a worldview value. Rather, Korean-American Christians find solidarity with Korean Buddhists, atheists, and even Korean Communists in the Confucian emphasis that children

---

[84] Park, *Racial Conflict and Healing*, pp. 125-126.

should take care of the 100 per cent of the financial needs of their parents.

The important lesson to take way from this chapter is the fact that all Korean-American families function from the Confucian standpoint and not from the standpoint of individualistic philosophy that pervades white Americans, regardless of their religion.[85] Confucianism is not only the central guiding principle for the Korean-American family, it is the only guiding principle. This is the case for every devout, Fundamentalist Baptist Christians among Korean-Americans as well as for Christianity-hating Buddhist Koreans in the Korean-American community. Confucian philosophy is the guiding philosophical principle and worldview dominating the direction of the Korean-American family and not the Renaissance-born philosophy of individualism that permeates through western countries, including America, which relegates the obligation to take care of the parents in their old age to the national government and its social security programs. Korean Christians actually criticize all white Christians as breaking the Ten Commandments' obligation to honor one's parents by not preaching support of their parents with 100 per cent financial support after retirement. Even Korean exegesis of the Ten Commandments is driven by Confucian philosophy and worldview, rather than western philosophy of individualism and western worldview regarding family.

Thus, it is clear that the Korean-American family is the most important Korean-American social unit. Although often integrated into the Korean-American church as the Confucian value-system is explained in light of the Christian Scriptures of the Old Testament and the New Testament, the Korean-American family retains the essential characteristics of the Confucian philosophical system which has undergirded the Korean society for over 1,500 years. Thus, without understanding the Confucian foundations of the Korean-American family, it is impossible to understand the

---

[85] Chang, " Communication and Acculturation," p. 146.

workings of the Korean-American family and identities attached to the Korean-American family.

Chapter 5:
"Korean-American Youths, the American Work Place, and US Politics"

The majority of the Korean-American youths in the United States of America were born in the USA. Majority of them do not have a first hand knowledge of Korea and have never lived in Korea. They know Korea only through their parents and through the medium of the Korean-American church. Their perception of what is Korean is colored by what is taught as Korean by their parents and their Korean-American church. Surprisingly enough, most Korean-American youth see themselves as Korean, rather than American, and they treasure their Korean identity far more than their American identity. But this is not uncommon in the American context, most people of color do not see themselves as Americans, primarily. This is true of Mexican-Americans as well as it is of Chinese-Americans and Vietnamese-Americans. They see themselves first and foremost as Mexican, Chinese, and Vietnamese, despite the fact that they are born in the United States. Many white Americans (whether they are Jewish, Muslim, Christian, or atheist) do not understand this reality among the people of color. The question rises: What are the factors contributing to the perception of Korean identity among Korean-Americans born in the United States? A part of the answer to this question was given in other chapters of this book, but we will discuss the issue more in detail. Understanding the Korean identity of Korean-American youths born in the United States will help better understand the attitude of Korean-American youths toward the United States of America.

There are several reasons why Korean-American youth perceive themselves primarily in terms of Korean identity. Most of the reasons relate to the self-awareness as a people of color. Whether they consciously acknowledge it or not, they are impacted negatively throughout their lives because they are a people of color. As Korean-American teenagers grow, they come to understand the issue of color more clearly and in terms of their own personal experiences.

The negative experiences resulting from their identity as a people of color are felt in every aspect of their lives – personal, professional, and social associations. Let me explain the situation. Personally, Korean-American teenagers experience rejection all the time based on the color of their skin. Korean-American teenagers rarely talk about the situation among themselves because it is just too depressing. Who would want to sit around and talk about how one is treated like a "loser" even if the fault is not hers? Even if they cannot change the color of their skin and white American teenagers who are discriminating against them are at fault, many Korean-American teenagers implicitly feel shame and embarrassment and they do not want to talk about it, even among Korean-American friends. This does not mean that they are not aware of the situation and deep inside they do not know what is going on. Korean-American teenagers know but often pretend like there is nothing wrong because they are trying to protect themselves against depression and discouragement. It is difficult enough having to fight through the white American world, they do not want to be bogged down by depression stemming from reflection of how they are personally discriminated against because of the color of their skin, which they cannot change.

It is a practical self-defensive mechanism, really. But it is not necessarily helpful for the long run. It is true that they cannot change the color of their skin, but examining and dissecting the causes and the structure of discrimination against Korean-Americans can help Korean-Americans understand their environment better. And in the long-run, Korean-American youth will be able to handle the situation much more constructively than just pretend like this does not exist when they know it exists. Unfortunately for the Korean-American community, there are not many places that would allow a corporate discussion of the discrimination against Korean-Americans. The place best suited for such a discussion is the Korean-American church. However, the problem is that the Korean-American church has ignored the discrimination against Korean-American youth in the larger context of the American society.

The reason for this is simple. The majority of the Korean-American church leadership are still first generation Koreans who have never gone through the American educational system. They just do not know what it is to study as a Korean-American in the public school system or in an American college. Their reference points are outside of America. Thus, many Korean-American church leaders just do not know and their ignorance impedes their effective leadership to discuss the problems and treat the effects of discrimination that Korean-American youth experience. The same problem exists at home. Most of the parents of Korean-American youth have not gone through the American educational system, so they do not know what it is like for a Korean-American student in a largely white or non-Korean setting. They do not even understand the general problems that teenagers in America face and what American public school system is like. Knowing neither the context nor the specifics of the discrimination against Korean-American youth, parents often think that there is not a problem. Since Korean-American youth are reluctant to talk about the discrimination that they have experienced even with their Korean-American friends, they will keep their suffering a secret from their parents. They figure that their parents cannot change their skin color, either. And having grown up in America, they may feel sensitive about saying something that may seem like a complaint on Korean ethnicity. So, trying not to hurt their parents' feelings, many Korean-American youth keep things bottled up and in the long-run this produces a very unhealthy effect.

But it is important to note that negative experiences stemming from being a people of color is not confined to the personal realm but is evidenced in the professional realm. Won Moo Hurh writes: "Overqualification for their jobs or underutilization of their education (underemployment) has been the most serious occupational problem for both native- and foreign-born Asian Americans."[86] Korean-Americans suffer real, quantifiable loss in the professional realm[87] as the result of discrimination of white bosses (whether these whites are Jewish, Muslim, Christian, or atheist) in the work place – who have an issue with the visible difference of Korean-Americans as a people of color.[88] The biggest problem in this regard are all the lies attached to the discrimination. Although white bosses (whether these whites are Jewish, Muslim, Christian, or atheist) are discriminating against Korean-American employees and passing them up for important promotions or even firing them unfairly, it is always described in politically correct terms or with other legitimate-sounding excuses.[89] Thus, although the employer knows he is discriminating against the Korean-American employee for being a person of color (or for being Korean, specifically), and the Korean-American employee knows this herself, it is never spoken about in those terms. This adds to the perception of Korean-American community members that they suffer double whammy

---

[86] Won Moo Hurh, "The 1.5 Generation: A Cornerstone of the Korean-American Ethnic Community," *The Emerging Generation of Korean-Americans*, eds. Ho-Youn Kwon and Shin Kim (Seoul: Kyung Hee University Press, 1993, pp. 47-79), p. 66.

[87] Won Moo Hurh, "Comparative Study of Korean Immigrants in the United States: A Typology," *Korean Christian Scholars Journal* 2 (Spring, 1977, p. 60-99), p. 81.

[88] There is still much research needed in this realm. The fact that Shinyoung Lee completely ignores this dimension is deplorable (Lee, *Impact of Ethnic Identity*, p. 33).

[89] Shin Kim, "Career Prospects of Korean Immigrants' Children," *The Emerging Generation of Korean-Americans*, eds. Ho-Youn Kwon and Shin Kim (Seoul: Kyung Hee University Press, 1993, pp. 107-123), p. 117.

injustice; they are discriminated and the discrimination is hidden under the rug.

Let me give a very common example. A Korean-American who came to America at a young age and has an accent goes to Harvard University to receive his bachelor's degree in physics. He then goes onto Stanford University to pursue a Ph.D. in physics. When he is done with his Ph.D. with distinction, he finds that he cannot procure a teaching job in a physics department anywhere in the United States. He is puzzled because he received his education from the best universities in America. He has proven himself academically, so he is wondering what went wrong. There are a few possibilities of what went wrong. During the course of his Ph.D., the Korean-American could have "rubbed the white people the wrong way." Most of his professors in the Physics Department will be white, although practically half of the Ph.D. students may be of Asian descent. The problem, of course, for the Korean-American is that he needs the recommendation letters of the white professors in his department at Stanford University. Because he offended white sensibilities of some of the faculty members who may be completely ignorant about Korean-American culture and his visible Koreanness, they will write him a bad recommendation. Thus, while white Ph.D.'s in his department who are actually inferior to him academically are getting good jobs, this Korean-American cannot even get one teaching post with a Ph.D. from Stanford. This may seem like a far out scenario for people who do not know what is going on in American universities, but this is a fairly common occurrence. All one has to do is a simple study of recent Ph.D.'s in any elite university in America – Harvard, MIT, Stanford – and he will be able to confirm this case to be true, every time.

There is another reason why a qualified Korean-American with a Ph.D. from Stanford in physics may not get a single teaching job. When he goes for an interview – if he gets that far – they will notice that he has a slight accent. Even if he does not have an accent, they will notice that there are visible differences about him, which is natural because he is a product of the Korean-American culture and community and not of a white culture and white community (whether the white community is white Jewish, white Muslim, white Christian, or white atheist). This Koreanness at the interview will be a strike against him. And most likely, he will not get the job because most physics departments in the United States have a predominantly white faculty and they want to maintain whiteness, whether they are willing to admit that consciously or not.

Of course, the professor writing the "recommendation" will not let on that he has written the Korean-American a negative recommendation. And the colleges interviewing him will not say that they did not hire him because of his Korean-Americanness. All will be explained in politically correct terms. The interviewing college will say that he is "not the right fit." This is a generic way of dismissing a candidate without having to give the true reason. Generally, when a college representative says this, this means that they have a problem with his Koreannesss. This excuse is so typical as to be formulaic for faulting Korean-Americans for being too Korean. Of course, their standard of "too Korean" would be anything that is not completely white, so even many Bananas would be found to have faults. How can Korean-Americans be completely white even if they strive to be when their parents are Korean-American and they have a Korean-American reference point? It is humanly and socially impossible.

This Korean-American physics Ph.D. from Stanford University is no fool. Obviously he was smart enough to get into Harvard University and he was smart enough to get into Stanford University for a Ph.D. He understands what is going on. White academics do not want him in their elite white club of the "university professors," thus, white professors – both female and male – are blocking him, a Korean-American, out of the white university (in terms of professorship) and white academia. He understands that the excuse they are giving is a politically correct response to protect themselves and put the burden on him (that he is not a right fit). The Korean-American physics Ph.D. from Stanford University understands that he has been a double whammy victim – (1) of discrimination and (2) of politically correct cover-up.

Professional suffering as the result of color is not confined to the world of the university and academia. Many Korean-Americans throughout the United States suffer discrimination based on color in all kinds of professions. Won Moo Hurh writes: "In general, Asian Americans are excluded from positions of power and influence."[90] Another example of Korean-Americans suffering discrimination in the work place is in the area of consulting. Consulting firms and investment banks like Korean-Americans because Korean-Americans tend to be bright and hard-working. Managers like Korean-Americans because as entry level analysts, they will work very hard and in the end managers get all the credit. Thus, it is not surprising that many Korean-Americans get hired as entry level analysts at consulting firms. The problem is that this generally tends to be dead-end jobs for Korean-Americans.[91] There are exceptions, but they are so seldom and far in-between to be exceptions that prove the rule. What happens?

Korean-Americans from Yale University with a bachelors degree in economics will be hired on by a consulting firm for $45,000 per year with a two year contract. For a Korean-American of twenty-one years old, this may seem like a lot of money. Not only will he get paid $45,000, his travel expenses and food will be paid for. This seems like all his years of sleepless nights studying for college entrance exams and four years of sleepless nights studying at Yale University finally paid off. He is so eager to get instant gratification for all his hard work that he jumps at the chance. But $45,000 is not a lot of money in relative terms. A high school graduate who never goes to college, but joins the police department will be paid that amount (and more!) by the time he is in his mid-twenties. So will a college graduate who becomes

---

[90] Hurh, "The 1.5 Generation," p. 66.
[91] Hurh, "The 1.5 Generation," p. 69.

a teacher who has 3 month summer vacation. He has 3 months off, works only 40 hours per week, and he gets paid the same amount of money as an entry level analyst. The difference is that the police officer and the teacher will not be laid off because they are US government jobs, whereas consulting jobs are private sector jobs subject to volatilities of the private market. And in the private market, one of those volatilities is that Korean-Americans get laid off, fired or have contracts not renewed because of the industry discrimination against Korean-Americans.[92]

Generally, a highly competent college graduate is given a contract for 2-year period to be an entry level analyst for the consulting firm. He will be paid at $45,000 plus benefits and possible bonuses. But his job is guaranteed only for 2 years. He will have to have his contract renewed after the end of the 2-year period or he has to move onto another job. At the age of 22, graduating from Yale University, a typical Korean-American does not know the American white corporate world. He thinks that this is a sweet deal and that he will be assured of a job after two years. In most cases, he assumes wrong. The white corporate world is not like Yale University where if one is a sophomore, one will become a junior. Contract renewals are more difficult than getting into Yale University from high school with a straight "A" grade *for* a person of color. But most Korean-Americans, especially if they talk with white individuals who are not subject to the color dilemma, think that it is a cakewalk to go from end of a two year contract to the renewal of that contract at a higher (or manager) pay. It just does not work that way for Korean-Americans, although it may work that way generally for white Americans.[93]

There are several reasons why Korean-Americans must face up to the realities of being the people of color. Most impor-

---

[92] Hurh, "The 1.5 Generation," pp. 71-72.
[93] Shin Kim, "Career Prospects of Korean Immigrants' Children," *The Emerging Generation of Korean-Americans*, eds. Ho-Youn Kwon and Shin Kim (Seoul: Kyung Hee University Press, 1993, pp. 107-123), p. 113.

tantly, a white employer will not fail to notice that a Korean-American is a person of color. He may ignore this fact or even forget this fact, but day in and day out, his white employer will not.[94] Thus, he starts out with a strike from the very beginning. More importantly from a practical standpoint, if a Korean-American does not recognize his vulnerability on account of being a person of color, he cannot adequately prepare for it. Thus, if the 2 year contract in a consulting firm is nearing completion, and a Korean-American guy wants to renew his contract, he needs to cater his preparation – imputing into his equation the important reality that he is a person of color and his chances of having his contract renewed is significantly minimized as a result. He may be successful with adequate preparation.

More importantly, he may explore other options in advance before it is too late. Thus, the Korean-Amrerican guy can apply for a MBA degree for instance in the beginning of his second year just in case his contract will not be renewed. This way, he will have a safety back-up in the event that he is not allowed to continue working for his company in the third year. When his white boss tells him that his contract will not be renewed and he cannot negotiate his way through it, then he will at least know that he has a 2-year MBA program waiting for him, which will allow him to get more training and better certification so that he will not be sidetracked in his career. Furthermore, he will not be sitting around doing nothing professionally just because his contract is not renewed.

There are many examples of Korean-Americans, even those who were born in the USA, who received 3.7 in their GPA from a prestigious place like the University of California at Berkeley or Harvard, who did not have their contracts renewed and became unemployed. It is very hard to find a job once the contract is terminated. As a result, many Koreans waste 1-4 years doing practically nothing in the area of their profession at the crucial stage of

---

[94] Kim, "Career Prospects," p. 117.

their professional advancement (because their contract was not renewed). Of course, it is understandable that a period of depression is natural. But these Korean-Americans could have saved wasting all those years if they did not assume that their contracts would be renewed and planned for some contingencies. Often, Korean-Americans are put off guard because they see that most white Americans have their contracts renewed, including those white American employees whom they think is not as good as they in the job.[95] Thus, they assume that their contract will be renewed. This is a grave mistake. They must recognize that they are people of color, whereas white Americans are not. Korean-Americans are very vulnerable in the American society, whereas white Americans generally are not. In a way, it would not be a mistake to say that American society belongs to white Americans. Korean-Americans, as a people of color, are often perceived not to own the piece of the pie of white Americans.

Besides personal and professional realms, Korean-Americans experience discrimination as a people of color in social realms. Although there may be exceptions to this rule, they are few and far in-between that they prove the rule. And when one examines the exceptions, one often finds that the exceptions are for Uncle Toms, who function as token Asians to bring benefit or wealth to white Americans (whether they are white Jewish, white Muslim, white Christian, or white atheist). Thus, although they seem to enjoy social privileges, they function actually as traitors to their own ethnic communities. The Korean-American community, like any other communities of color, has its share of Uncle Toms.

What are the kinds of social disadvantages which Korean-Americans encounter on the basis of color? Korean-Americans are often excluded from social gatherings, especially as Korean-Americans get older. There is a reason why Korean-Americans sit together with other Asian-Americans at Harvard University during lunch time. It is not because they are all ignorant about American

---

[95] Kim, "Career Prospects," p. 118.

culture and do not know America. The majority of Korean-Americans going to elite universities in this country are American-born and very familiar with American ways. Of course, when one asks white students at Harvard University or elsewhere, they will say that Korean-Americans choose to segregate themselves. Although this may be true in some cases, it is not true generally. When asked, Korean-Americans prefer to have a mixture of Korean-American friends and friends from other ethnic backgrounds. In fact, after Korean-Americans, Korean-Americans prefer to have white friends in college. However, Korean-Americans are prevented socially from achieving their goal because they are ostracized, often politely and politically correctly. Exclusion can be very polite.

Social exclusion of this kind can take the form of floormates in a dormitory going out to a restaurant but somehow they "forgot" to tell the only Korean-American guy in the Freshman dorm floor. It can be invitations to parties or other weekend social functions not being extended to Korean-Americans. Certain college clubs do not announce aggressively for fear that Korean-American students will flock and join the group, thereby shifting the balance of power in the group from white to Asian. There are many other forms of social exclusion, and it is based primarily on the fact that Korean-Americans are a people of color. Even the most "Americanized" Korean-Americans seem to have a problem with social acceptance by white individuals (Jewish, Muslim, Christian, or atheist) and white groups (secular or religious).

But social exclusion of Korean-Americans in terms of friendship and friendship groups is not the only form of social discrimination that Korean-Americans experience on the basis of their color. Korean-Americans often experience social discrimination in social groupings in the context of the work place. It is common knowledge that Americans often form their friendships in the context of the workplace. Co-workers have lunch together and often meet up after the work is over for social outings or other fun activities. Forming friendships with people at work is a very American thing. Still, in many countries, work is work and private life is private life. People keep these two spheres separate, and they consciously work to keep these two spheres apart.

In the American context, because friendships form in the context of the work place, work/personal division becomes blurred. Often, one finds that co-workers are the closest "friends" in terms of being confidants and individuals that people rely on in times of need. Co-workers seem to know more about a typical American in question than even their parents. The mixing of the personal realm and the work realm has made America an interesting social experiment. For Korean-Americans and other people of color, this mixing has proved to be detrimental.

White Americans are raised with a certain set of expectations in the white American cultural setting. They may never question these set of expectations and guidelines, but they exist and they are distinctively white. In other words, there are mores and customs in white American cultural contexts which white Americans take for granted, which are not a part of the cultures of the people of color. This is not surprising because almost all of the people of color originally came from non-western, non-European cultural settings. Furthermore, the people of color in the American context have suffered discrimination, slavery, and injustice perpetrated, maintained, and defended by white communities (Jewish, Christian, atheist, or other). Thus, even if they inhabit the same geographic space, white Americans and Americans of color do not share common set of cultural values or the same perception about institutions, realities, and internalized white American culture. Just because people are not openly talking about it does not mean that serious social rifts do not exist.

In the context of the professional work place, friendships among co-workers have become very important. Small chit-chats are expected. Co-workers are expected to share the most intimate details of their personal lives. Every day, co-workers expect to hear some new developments in the personal lives of those with whom they work. This is clearly brought out in American movies.

When one compares American movies and European movies, one notices a very important difference in the way co-workers relate to each other. In America, it is assumed that one's co-workers will be one's friends, and if not, they will be his enemies. The American workplace does not exist as a neutral social realm or as a purely work-oriented space. The important fact is that American workplaces do not strive for neutrality. The American workplace is what it is because Americans want it that way. And by Americans, we mean white Americans (whether they are Jewish, Christian, or other) because whites have built and established the nature and character of the American workplace for hundreds of years. People of color were not allowed to participate in a typical work place until very recently – only a few decades ago. So, the people of color really did not have such a significant contribution to the nature and character of the American workplace. Even today, in professional work settings, people of color tend to be relatively invisible vis-à-vis white Americans. Thus, even today, white Americans dictate the nature and character of the American workplace.

Because white Americans shape and direct the nature and character of the American workplace – whether consciously or not – the people of color are by definition vulnerable in the context of the defining and re-defining of the American workplace by white Americans who share a similar Eurocentric culture, history, and mores. Thus, when an unspoken rule exists for co-workers to be friends and to share intimate personal details, this disadvantages the people of color. Korean-Americans are no exception. In fact, Korean-Americans become highly vulnerable. There are several reasons why Korean-Americans may be more vulnerable than other communities of color.

First of all, Korean-American culture is diametrically opposed to Eurocentric white American culture. For instance, the Korean-American cultural mandate to support one's parents with 100 per cent financial assistance will not be understood by white Americans – Jewish, Christian or other. And the response will be highly negative when they hear this personal side of Korean-

Americans. Some white Americans may feel guilty because they do not even support their parents financially at all by choice. They may hate Korean-Americans for being "goody-goody." And everyone who has been to an American high school knows how "goody-goody" are treated in high school. The Korean-American can be hated by white Americans in their heart just because they are being Korean-Americans in the way most Korean-Americans are. What is normal and common in the Korean-American culture is completely opposed to the common practice of white Americans.

The problem for Korean-Americans is that the difference hurts Korean-Americans in the predominantly white American work place. Older Americans in the workplace may feel jealousy. If they find out that Korean-Americans support their parents with 100 per cent financial support and they are nearing retirement age, they will be very jealous. Especially if they have not saved up enough for retirement, that jealousy can take the form of a real hatred against Korean-Americans. Obviously, since everyone is expected to share personal aspects of their lives in the white American workplace, Korean-Americans share personal details about their lives, which are typical and common in the Korean-American culture, not knowing that it will draw guilt-ridden hatred and jealousy-compelled hatred against them. And of course, hatred does not end in the person's heart; it will result in social consequences. Those white Americans who harbor hatred in their hearts against the Korean-American who has merely shared a personal detail about his life which is typically Korean-American can find himself in a situation where white Americans are consciously trying to undermine him at work and sabotage his career. Office politics takes on a completely new dimension for the Korean-American and one of the greatest tragedies associated with this whole story is that the Korean-American is probably not aware of why all the negative things are happening to him. Those white Americans whom he considers as his friends in the work place have developed secret hatred against him based on practices that are common to the Korean-American culture. And this hatred will cost the Korean-American his promotion and potentially even his job as well.

Unlike Korean-Americans who may not be aware of what is going on, the experience is completely different for African-Americans. African-Americans have been slaves in America for hundreds of years. And as slaves of white Americans, African-Americans have developed an awareness of white American culture through the centuries, and this awareness has sensitized African-Americans to be instinctively cautious against "red flags" in white American culture. Thus, even the most uneducated African-American will know what ticking bombs to avoid vis-à-vis white Americans and the white American culture. They may intentionally choose to trespass the boundaries, but they know white boundaries exist and basically know what they are. Korean-Americans are happily and perhaps haplessly oblivious. And this costs Korean-Americans in serious ways.

Korean-Americans as a community are still very ignorant about white America. This is clear when one reads Korean-American newspapers and even Korean-American publications in English. There is hardly any discussion of Korean-American culture as it stands apart from the white American culture. If one asks a very educated Korean-American what a white culture is, not only will he not be able to tell you what it is, he may not even be aware that there is such a thing. He may have suffered overt discrimination by white Americans as many Korean-Americans have, but he will merely stamp on the title "racist" for that white individual without exploring the complex dimensions of the American society. It is always simpler and easier to call someone a racist and dismiss him rather than work to understand the nature of white America and the complex relationship between the Korean-American culture and white Americans. And the lazy route is what most Korean-Americans have chosen to take in regards to discrimination against Korean-Americans. The problem is that the lazy route of name calling is not constructive to problem solving or protection of Korean-Americans in white America.

One of the reasons for such ignorance is due to non-participation in the politics of the United States. Korean-Americans are thought to be very apathetic to American politics. Even those who have been politically very active in Korea tend to exhibit political nonchalance regarding U.S. politics. In fact, many Korean-Americans do not vote in local, state, or national elections of the United States of America.[96] In contrast, Korean-American parents often exhibit strong interest in Korean politics. Sunok Chun Pai writes: "Even though they left Korea, or probably because of it, Koreans are fiercely patriotic or nationalistic to Korea."[97]

An important factor that discourages Korean-American involvement is due to the perception that the United States of America stands against the unification of South Korea and North Korea. One factor perpetuating this notion is the propaganda of North Korea. North Korea has demanded complete removal of U.S. Armed Forces from the Korean peninsula as a prerequisite to adopting any declaration of non-aggression by North Korea and signing a peace agreement between North Korea and the United States to replace the Armistice Treaty of 1953.[98] North Korea seems earnest in their proposition. More importantly, such a request jives with the sentiment of Koreans in South Korea. Although the South Korean government has agreed to U.S. troop presence in South Korea as a form of deterrence against North Korean aggression, the majority of Koreans in the South perceive the U.S. military presence as a hindrance to the Unification Process. Tae-Hwan Kwak writes: "Without mutual concessions and compromise between top deci-

---

[96] Chai, "The Korean-American Community and U.S. Politics," p. 94.
[97] Sunok Chun Pai, "The Changing Role of Korean-Americans," *The Emerging Generation of Korean-Americans*, eds. Ho-Youn Kwon and Shin Kim (Seoul: Kyung Hee University Press, 1993, pp. 215-224), p. 218.
[98] Tae-Hwan Kwak, "The Role of the Korean-American Community in Peacemaking Process on the Korean Peninsula," *The Korean-American Community: Present and Future*, eds. Tae-Hwan Kwak and Seong Hyong Lee (Seoul: Kyungnam University Press, 1991, pp. 99-112), p. 101.

sion-makers of both sides, one cannot expect a durable peace on the Korean peninsula and the peaceful unification of Korea."[99] And Chai adds: "In the peace making process on the Korean peninsula, the Seoul government needs seriously consider the long-term strategic planning about U.S. troop withdrawal issue and have serious discussions on this issue with the U.S. government."[100] The concern for the unification of South Korea and North Korea is all-encompassing in the Korean-American community, including the Korean-American Church. Yong Choon Kim expresses a popular value among Korean-American Christians: "As a spiritual and moral leader of the Korean-American community, the Korean Presbyterian churches in North America should take a leading role to make an outstanding contribution even for the unification of the motherland, which is a long-awaited and perennial hope and the most important task of the Korean people. Korean-American churches should not only pray for this task, but also make a strong effort and play an active leading role for the early fulfilment of this national wish."[101]

Furthermore, a lack of interest in American politics is further fuelled by the growing awareness in the Korean community that the United States not only did not directly intervene to end Japanese Occupation against Koreans, many of whom were Christians, but also that the United States sold Korea out. In 1905, Prime Minister Taro Katsura of Japan and William Howard Taft, U.S. Secretary of War, signed the Taft-Katsura Agreement which allowed Japanese annexation of Korea in exchange for Japan not objecting to U.S. rule in the Philippines.[102]

Although Korean-American youth, like their parents, may not critically question the workings of the American society and white Americans, they have experienced discrimination in personal,

---

[99] Kwak, "The Role of the Korean-American Community," p. 101.
[100] Kwak, "The Role of the Korean-American Community," p. 108.
[101] Kim, "The Protestant Church and the Korean-American Community," p. 209.
[102] Andrew Sung Park, *Racial Conflict and Healing: An Asian-American Theological Perspective* (Maryknoll: Orbis Books, 1996), p. 12.

professional, and social settings where white Americans dominate, particularly in positions of power. What does this mean in terms of Korean-American youth and their perception of the United States of America? With the simple label "racist," Korean-American youth are developing hatred of the United States of America. Unlike their parents who tend to be aggressively pro-American and join the Republican Party, Korean-American youth tend to blame the US government for the racism that they experience in the personal, professional, and social realms, and they typically join the Democratic Party and vote for Democratic candidates whom they perceive as most critical of America and American government policies. Thus, we can even now speak about the generation gap in the Korean-American community as a political gap. Among the Korean-Americans who vote, Korean-American parents are mostly Republicans and vote for pro-American politicians, and their children are mostly Democrats and vote for politicians critical of American policies around the world and in domestic matters.

    A more nuanced understanding of the complexities of culture and the workings of white Americans along their diachronic and synchronic realities will anchor Korean-Americans against out-right anti-Americanism based on the simple label of "white racism" without content or understanding. Not all patriotic Americans are racist, and not all Americans critical of American policies love Asian-Americans. It is far more complex than that. Understanding the boundaries of the white American culture and white American perceptions will stem the growing tide of blatant anti-Americanism that is sweeping across the Korean-American youth culture.

Chapter 6:
"The Korean-American Conflict with African-Americans"

Although Korean-Americans may not be aware of their conflict with white America and white Americans (whether they are Jewish, atheist, Christian, or Muslim whites), they are hyper-aware of their conflicts with African-Americans. In fact, there is not a Korean-American who is not aware of the conflict with African-Americans. The awareness of the Korean-American conflict with African-Americans exists at every level of the Korean-American society throughout all the states of the United States of America, regardless of class, education, background, gender, sexual orientation, and religion.

There are several reasons for the communal consciousness of the Korean-American conflict with African-Americans. First of all, the Los Angeles Riots in 1992 after the acquittal of the policemen who beat Rodney King confirmed in most Korean-American minds the deep hatred that African-Americans have for Korean-Americans.[103] The question that rose after the beating of Rodney King by white police officers was: If black Americans are angry with white police for their discrimination against blacks, then why don't the black people go to white shops and destroy them and wreak havoc on white communities? The fact that African-Americans targeted Korean shops and the Koreatown for their protest against whites proved in the Korean-American communal mind that African-Americans hate Korean-Americans more than anybody else, even those who actually inflict harm on them.

---

[103] Andrew Sung Park, *Racial Conflict and Healing: An Asian-American Theological Perspective* (Maryknoll: Orbis Books, 1996), p. 29.

There are thousands of Korean shop owners who were destroyed because of the Los Angeles Riots, and Korean-Americans were primary victims of the African-American protest in Los Angeles against white police and the discriminatory white infrastructure. Korean-Americans still feel a deep-seated resentment for being the scapegoats for African-American angst and protest.[104] It will be difficult to find a Korean-American in Los Angeles today who has forgiven the African-American community for what they have done. As Christians, most Korean-Americans try to act in friendship and Korean-American pastors have encouraged reconciliation between Korean-American Christians and African-American Christians who share the same religion, but most Korean-Americans do this reluctantly. And Korean-American pastors who have arranged for Christian fellowship between a Korean-American church and an African-American church have been fired from their pastoral positions before such a meeting could take place. The major bone of contention among Korean-Americans is that the Korean-American community has suffered too great a loss and the memory is still so very fresh that it would be disrespectful to those who have been ruined by the Los Angeles Riots, who still go to Korean-American churches to make any gesture of joint fellowship. They feel that it should be African-American churches which take the position of being sorry and extend the hand of friendship for encouraging such an attack on Korean-American shopkeepers, and not the other way around.

The Korean-American resentment against African-Americans is deep not only in the Los Angeles area. One of the reasons for this problem is that Los Angeles is not the only area where Korean-American merchants suffered. There were two major African-American boycotts of Korean-American businesses in

---

[104] Shin Kim, "Conceptualization of Inter-Minority Group Conflict: Conflict between Korean Entrepreneurs and Black Local Residents," *The Korean-American Community: Present and Future* (Seoul: Kyungnam University Press, 1991, pp. 29-48), p. 44.

New York City in 1980s. First one was organized by New York Harlem residents in 1984-1985. The boycott started after an African-American customer who was having an argument with a Korean-American store owner was arrested by the police. The boycott lasted six months. The second boycott started in July, 1988, and lasted until February, 1989. This boycott was conducted by Brooklyn's African-Americans and targeted Korean businesses in New York City. This boycott started after an altercation between a Korean-American store owner and an African-American customer who was accused of theft.[105] Many New York Korean-American businesses suffered as the result of these two major boycotts.

But the conflict is not confined to Korean-American store owners and African-American customers. There is conflict between Korean-American business owners and African-American employees. Generally, Korean-Americans have hired Mexican-Americans. For instance, in Los Angeles only 6.5% of Korean-American businesses hired one or more African-American employees, whereas 40.4% hired one or more Mexican-American employees. There is a perception among Los Angeles Korean-American businesses that Mexican-Americans are harder working and more reliable than African-American employees.[106] However, recognizing that hiring African-American employees is good for public relations, many Korean-American businesses have started to hire more African-Americans. But with increased hiring came increasing mistrust. Korean-American employers became frustrated by frequent absentee of some of the African-American employees. Some Korean-American businesses state that frequent complaints by African-American employees were unreasonable. Other Korean-American business owners complained about theft among African-American employees, many of whom were from the

---

[105] Pyong Gap Min, "Korean Immigrants' Small Business Activities and Korean-Black Interracial Conflicts," *The Korean-American Community: Present and Future*, eds. Tae-Hwan Kwak and Seong Hyong Lee (Seoul: Kyungnam University Press, 1991, pp. 13-28), p. 18.
[106] Min, "Korean Immigrant's Small Business Activities," pp. 21-22.

neighborhood of the business and were economically depressed.[107] Because as immigrants, Korean-Americans were juggling several big bank loans (house, business, and car), what Korean-American store owners perceive as African-American inefficiency and loss of profit due to that seriously irritate Korean-American store owners. This, in turn, does not help the relationship between Korean-American store owners and their African-American employees.

Throughout the United States of America, most Korean-American churches still cannot extend the hand of friendship to African-American churches for fear that they will alienate their church members who are still very bitter about the Los Angeles Riots. The fact that hardly any African-American church has made the first step to develop friendships with Korean-American churches serves as proof-positive that African-Americans feel no remorse for the Los Angeles Riots and the persecution of Korean-Americans by African-Americans. The resentment against African-Americans can be seen to exist not only among church goers but also among many Korean-American pastors. There are still some Korean-American pastors making a concerted effort to develop friendships between the two communities, but they are often resented by the Korean-American community and its members. For instance, Korean Brooklyn Church initiated a joint Christian worship service between Korean-Americans and African-Americans in 1984 in response to the first African-American boycott of Korean-American businesses in New York.[108] But this program has been discontinued due to lack of support from the Korean-American community in New York City. Most pastors who have actually held joint fellowship programs between Korean-Americans and African-Americans have seen their church mem-

---

[107] Shin Kim, "Coceptualization of Inter-Minority Group Conflict," pp. 39-40.
[108] Chong Sik Ahn, "An Alternative Approach to the Racial Conflict between Korean-American Small Business Owners and the Black-American Community in the New York Metropolitan Area," *The Korean-American Community: Present and Future*, eds. Tae-Hwan Kwak and Seong Hyong Lee (Seoul: Kyungnam University Press, 1991, pp. 49-55), p. 53.

bership drop below 50 per cent after the start of the joint fellowship programs. Some Korean pastors experiencing fall in their church membership resulting from Korean-American resentment often give up their attempt to reach out to African-American Christians. Those who continue despite the fall in church membership do so on ideological grounds that it is the right thing for Korean-American Christians and African-American Christians to share Christian brotherhood in the blood of Jesus Christ.

The situation is not improving in this regard. The Korean-American community's resentment against African-Americans is at an all time high right now. And it seems that the resentment is growing with each generation. Korean-American youth of today are politically correct and are friendly to African-Americans on the surface, but they actually hate African-Americans far more than their parents. Their parents tend to be very Korean and show how they feel inside. So, they may harbor little resentment which shows itself in very visible ways. The children, born in America and educated in the American educational system, developed the American way of hiding their true feeling and showing politically correct "friendship." The strongest evidence of deep seated hatred of African-Americans among Korean-American youth is found in the fact that it is the Korean-American youth who most aggressively protest having any joint fellowship meetings with African-American churches. While there are many joint fellowships between Korean-born Korean-American adults and African-Americans, such joint fellowships are rare between Korean-American church youth groups and African-American church youth groups. Furthermore, when their parents lead a joint fellowship between Korean-Americans and African-Americans, Korean-American youth are often conspicuously missing from the joint fellowships.

On one level, it may be understandable why Korean-American youth resent African-Americans more than their parents. First of all, Korean-American parents generally have a greater exposure to African-Americans on a daily basis. This may be surprising but it really is not when one examines the development of the Korean-American community in the United States. The majority of the Korean-American parents say that they immigrated to the United States for their children's education. This being the goal, most Korean-Americans prioritize placing their family in a good school district as the most important. It happens to be that good school districts tend to be all white or predominantly white. Thus, Korean-American families move into white neighborhoods relatively early on in their immigration history. Although Korean-Americans do all they could to put their children in good educational neighborhoods, they do not focus on moving their work place to white neighborhoods. Korean-Americans have no problem working in an African-American neighobrhood and do not see that as necessarily disadvantageous. In this sense, Korean-Americans can be characterized as a racially tolerant people. They move to an all white neighborhood for the sake of their children's education although it is easier to live among Korean people, and they do not make an effort to move out of a workplace in the African-American neighborhood as long as the work pays the bills. Korean-Americans will never move their work to a white neighborhood even if they make 100 dollars less in a white neighborhood. For the sake of saving up for children's college education, Korean-American parents will stay in the African-American neighborhood if they will make 100 dollars more. Thus, many Korean-American parents work in predominantly African-American neighborhoods and deal mostly, if not exclusively, with black customers on a day to day basis. But their children will be placed in a good school district as soon as possible, so most Korean-American youth will rarely have exposure to African-Americans who tend to be conspicuously missing from the best educational districts in every state of the United States of America. African-American demographics are changing to be sure; however, this scenario is still relatively true in most places.

  Besides relative lack of exposure to African-Americans, another reason why Korean-American youth resent African-

Americans more than their Korean-American parents is that Korean-American youth are educated in America whereas Korean-American parents tend to have some of their education in Korea. Why does this even make a difference? When Korean textbooks on American history teach slavery, there is an outright condemnation of white slave owners. It is a black and white ethical issue and Korean textbooks on slavery moralize against slavery. In a way, it is an easy thing for Korean textbooks to do. It was not the ancestors of Koreans who enslaved the black people. They have no stake in the condemnation. In contrast, most American textbooks gloss over the slavery period or ignore the horrors of slavery. Certainly, there will not be a moralizing condemnation of the slavery period in a typical American history textbook. Young Pai writes: "But since the core values of the so-called American culture are defined in terms of the value orientation of the White-Anglo-Saxon-Protestant (WASP) tradition, we need to reconsider seriously the proper role of the American school if cultural pluralism is to be realized in this country."[109] The fact is that these textbooks are written by white Americans, many of whom feel guilty about the past and their guilty feelings prevent them from an outright condemnation of slavery.

Other whites have another agenda. They want to end affirmative action or they have some grudge against present-day African-Americans and the African-American community for whatever reason and their resentment fuels silence in the condemnation of hundreds of years of slavery. And it is important to understand that not only are textbooks written by white Americans mostly, history courses are taught predominantly by white Americans in America's public schools, which means that their white prejudices even regarding the slavery period will show through.[110] Korean-Americans are taught American history by white teachers at their

---

[109] Young Pai, "Cultural Pluralism and American Education," *Korean Christian Scholars Journal* 2 (Spring, 1977, pp. 100-125), p. 103.
[110] Pai, "Cultural Pluralism and American Education," pp. 104-105.

formative, non-critical thinking periods and assimilate their foundational perception about African-Americans along white American lines.[111] Thus, it is their American high school education that cements the bias against African-Americans. Korean-American youth are, after all, a product of American education and not a Korean educational system. Thus, it is understandable why Korean-American youth tend to be far more biased against the African-American community than their Korean-American parents are.

Thirdly, Korean-American youth tend to be more anti-African-American than their parents because of their perception that African-Americans hate their parents and persecute them. Although most Korean-American youth go to schools in good school districts which tend to be very white, their parents tend to work in predominantly or exclusively black neighborhoods. For instance, 44% of total Korean-American businesses in Atlanta had mostly African-American customers because these businesses were located in African-American neighborhoods.[112] Korean-Americans often play the middlemen between depressed African-American neighborhoods and corporate America which is reluctant to bring superior goods and services into depressed African-American neighborhoods. Big Corporations are not willing to enter these African-American neighborhoods because of a high crime rate and a low profit margin.[113] Being the high crime areas that they are, it is not surprising for many Korean-American businesses in such economically depressed areas to experience frequent incidences of crime.

Every Korean-American merchant in the African-American community knows of a Korean-American merchant who has been robbed at gun point at some point in their decades of working in the neighborhood.[114] Many know of Korean-American merchants

---

[111] Pai, "Cultural Pluralism and American Education," p. 111.
[112] Min, "Korean Immigrants' Small Business Activities," p. 16.
[113] Min, "Korean Immigrants' Small Business Activities," p. 17.
[114] Kim, "Conceptualization of Inter-Minority Group Conflict," p. 30.

who have been shot, and some even those Korean-Americans who have been killed. Because of the robbery and murder by African-American criminals, Korean-American youth develop a dislike of African-Americans from an early age. Of course, as they grow up, they understand that it is only the criminal elements in the African-American community and many African-Americans are decent people. But they develop this perception relatively late in life, typically beyond their teenage years. And head knowledge does not always equal how one feels. As children and even before the age of reason, Korean-Americans have heard of African-Americans robbing and killing Korean-American merchants. Thus, from an early age, they develop a dislike of African-Americans. The fact that their childhood notions are replaced by head knowledge in college does not mean that they will completely change the way they have felt about African-Americans growing up as children. Childhood memories and resentments often remain a lifetime. In contrast, Korean-American parents did not have the same experience because most of them were born in Korea and did not have their whole childhood colored by negative discourse regarding African-Americans that exists in the Korean-American community.

Fourthly, Korean-American youth harbor greater resentment against African-Americans than their parents because they have experienced rejection by African-Americans on a personal level. Korean-American parents generally tend to have Korean-American friends, and they are set in their Korean ways. Their relationship to non-Koreans tends to be on formal or business levels. Thus, a Korean-American shop owner in an African-American community will have African-American customers. Their relationship remains in the realm of business transactions. However, Korean-American youths spend their whole life in America. Even if many of the Korean-Americans may not come into contact with African-Americans going to a good high school in a good school district, many of them encounter African-Americans in college and in the work place. It is in these areas primarily where Korean-Americans experience personal rejection by African-Americans.

It is one of the greatest tragedies of American college life that African-Americans have traditionally rejected Asian-Americans as a fellow people of color and have been reluctant to befriend Korean-Americans. Even now, any contact between Asian-Americans and African-Americans is the result of the first step taken by Asian-Americans and not the other way around. One of the reasons why African-Americans have excluded Asian-Americans from people of color issues and movements is because African-American leaders tend to be ignorant about Asian-American history and do not have many Asian-American friends. Historically, Asian-Americans have been excluded by the same laws excluding African-Americans. In the South, the segregation was not along black-white lines, but rather along colored-white lines. This means that if a Chinaman were to go to the South during this period, the Chinaman was expected to go to the colored section and not the white section (such as in bathroom areas, inside the bus, and in other segregated areas) in a town or a city. In fact, the Chinese are called the blacks of the West or blacks of California because it was the Chinese who worked as coolie workers and laid the railroads. Although they were not called slaves because they started their work after the end of the Civil War, for all intents and purposes, they engaged in a slave-type labor with a slave-type pay. There is a serious resentment among Asian-Americans because African-Americans have failed generally to recognize the suffering of Asian-Americans as a people of color in the United States of America. Most Asian-Americans feel betrayed by the African-American community and its communal leaders. In college, African-American student groups do not invite Asian-American student groups in activities that relate to people of color issues. Generally, African-American student groups in college do not extend an official invitation to Asian-American student groups for joint programs. Korean-Americans, like other Asian-Americans, feel a deep sense of rejection by African-American student groups in universities. The fact that African-Americans often poke fun of Asian-Americans when they do not give equal time to poking fun of the whites confirm the personal experiences of Korean-Americans. Thus, Korean-American youth's resentment against African-Americans is more pro-active and stronger in nature than that of their parents.

Another reason that contributes to the resentment by Korean-American youth toward African-Americans is what happens in the realm of American politics. Most Korean-American parents do not really care about American politics. They register themselves as Republicans and generally vote Republican during elections, but they do not spend much time following American politics. In fact, most Korean-American parents will follow Korean politics on a daily basis, and they will know intimate details of what's going on in Korean politics in South Korea. But most Korean-American youth do not care at all about Korean politics. Many of them were born in the United States and they have been completely educated in the USA. As they grow older, they develop interest in American politics and many tend to join the Democratic Party with critical attitudes toward the US government. Many of the politically conscientious Korean-American youth tend to feel a sense of solidarity with African-American politicians and their attitudes towards US policies. In fact, it would not be inaccurate to say that out of all the Democratic politicians, Korean-American youth will tend to agree most with African-American elected officials and the values that they represent. They can identify with the color issues. They can identify on being critical of US government policies. For instance, when the War on Iraq was being started, Korean-American youth predominantly sided with black politicians opposing the war against Iraq. Whereas the US military saw an upsurge of whites signing up in days leading up to war against Iraq, it did not see similar percentage rise among African-Americans and Asian-Americans.

Although Korean-American youth agree most with African-American politicians' positions on domestic and global issues,

African-Americans have not supported Asian-American advancement in the Democratic Party. African-American politicians generally do not want to hire Asian-Americans to work with them in their political campaigns and as an integral part of their political team. In contrast, white politicians have been relatively welcoming of Asian-American involvement in their political campaigns and invited quite a number of Korean-Americans to joint their team. The fact that African-American politicians do not seem to encourage Korean-American advancement in Democratic Party politics and in the political realm generally has created a disillusioned resentment against the African-American community as a whole among the Korean-Americans youth who support the Democratic Party. Thus, internally within Democratic Party politics, the resentment fuels Korean-American support of white candidates who oppose black candidates and white Democrats who oppose black Democrats on all kinds of issues, including during times white Democrats play dirty politics against black Democrats, like in recent days.

Korean-American youth are an integral part of the American society and as educated and thinking individuals, they make their decisions. However, like the African-American community members, Korean-Americans have suffered a lot for being a people of color in the personal, professional and social realms. Thus, Korean-Americans' intelligent choices and educated decisions are moderated by their personal experiences and feelings of pain and resentment. When African-Americans reject Korean-Americans and do not pro-actively embrace them in personal, professional, social, and political realms, Korean-American youth act out of their pain and suffering. Thus, it is not surprising that many Korean-American youth deeply dislike African-Americans more than their parents. They have experienced personal rejection more than their parents did. And unlike their parents, who do not really care about personal acceptance by African-Americans, Korean-Americans personally desire to be accepted by African-Americans and the African-American community. Because the situation does not seem to be changing, most likely the resentment among Korean-American youth against the African-American community will grow.

Heerak Christian Kim

Chapter 7:
"The Korean-American Youth Search for Group Identity"

It is not difficult to see why Asian-Americans, including Korean-Americans, are in the process of searching for identity. Asian-Americans experience rejection from the dominant white group (whether Christian, atheist, Jewish, Muslim, or other) and from the established African-American community. The rejection is on individual levels as they understand their experiences of rejection to be rejection of them personally by whites or blacks. But the sense of rejection is not merely on the individual level. Many Korean-Americans perceive that they are not only rejected from a bilateral relationship with whites and blacks on individual levels, they also feel that they are excluded from participating in white group activities and black group activities. Thus, search for individual identity is necessarily tied to a quest for a group identity.

It is true that in high school years that many Korean-Americans try to co-exist in the existent group structures. Thus, without real critical questioning, they flow with the mainstream of the high school and try to find a niche within that mainstream flow or in the peripheries of that flow. A part of the Korean-American problem is that there are not many Korean-Americans in high school settings. Even in areas with large Korean populations like Los Angeles, Koreans tend to be quite small in number relative to the larger context. 1.3 million Koreans in the greater Los Angeles region is a drop in the bucket because there are many more non-Koreans. In the State of Israel, Arabs comprise 20 per cent of the national population. It is possible to find cities which are predominantly Arabic, such as Nazareth. And even in historically

Jewish cities like Haifa, some estimate the Arab population at nearly 50 per cent. Such case does not exist in the United States for Korean-Americans. Wherever Korean-Americans are, they are a miniscule minority or a minority of minorities. Thus, in any given high school, Korean-Americans will be few in number. Paucity of the number of Korean-Americans in high schools often does not allow for a group identity as Korean-Americans. It would be hard for two or three Koreans to sit around and feel that they are actually Korean-Americans and that their group identity is a viable one. Thus, even within the mainstream flow of high school life, Korean-Americans mostly fail to establish a micro-group identity of Korean-Americans.

Korean-Americans have found another way to compensate for this problem. Some Korean-Americans have grouped themselves together with Chinese and Japanese Americans. Physically, there is no visible difference between Koreans, Chinese, and Japanese. If one does not speak, a Chinese person can be mistaken for a Korean or a Japanese. And this is the case for members of all three ethnic groups. Whereas the parents of Korean, Chinese, and Japanese students in high schools may speak the language of the Old Country primarily, this is just not the case for their children. Korean, Chinese, and Japanese youth in high school speak primarily in English. Many of them were born in the United States of America and have never been to the Old Country. They know Old Country only through pictures and from what they hear from their parents and ethnic social associations. For Korean-Americans, Chinese-Americans, and Japanese-Americans, they understand that their primary identity is attached to America. Interestingly enough, members of these three ethnic groups have unified and created an Asian identity. They call themselves Asians and prefer to have Asian friends. Often, they would subsume their particular ethnic identity (Korean, Chinese, or Japanese) under the pan-Asian identity.

It is important to understand why such a process is possible and even seen as desirable by many Korean-Americans, Chinese-

Americans, and Japanese-Americans in America's high schools. These youth reason that they are all alike in culture. Since they do not really understand the particulars of Korean, Chinese, and Japanese cultures, having been raised in America to parents who have lived in America for decades, they are not concerned with the specific details. Of course, there is a cultural gap between Koreans, Chinese, and Japanese in the Asian context, just as there are cultural gaps between the British, the French, and Germans in the European context. However, certainly there are more similarities uniting particular Asian ethnic individuals to Asians of other particular ethnicities within the group of Asians. In the same way, Germans, the French, and the British will find much more in common with each other than they would with Asians or Americans. Since there is greater commonality among Korean-Americans, Chinese-Americans, and Japanese-Americans, any way, and since the youth in this country who belong to these particular ethnic groups have been diluted in terms of their understanding and experience of their particular ethnic identity vis-à-vis their Old Country, which many of them have never even visited since birth, they feel comfortable drawing on a type of pan-Asian identity.

Of course, the paucity of the number of particular ethnicity (whether Korean, Chinese, or Japanese) does not hurt the process of amalgamation of a pan-Asian identity. One cannot find a significant number of Koreans in one high school. One cannot find a significant number of Chinese in one high school. One cannot find a significant number of Japanese in one high school. But one can find that all of them will comprise a significant number vis-à-vis the majority (whether white, black, or Hispanic) in a particular neighborhood. Often, Korean-Americans, Chinese-Americans, and Japanese-Americans opt to forge a group identity as Asian-Americans. Of course, this is often a passive process within the mainstream flow of their high school. Their high school has dominant identities and they form "friendship" and this becomes their functional group identity. They may not critically evaluate what they are doing or that they are forming a group identity, but certainly this is what is going on. It should be noted that some high schools do have conscious group identity formation by Asian-American youths. This would take the form of establishing a Asian-American Students Club or other types of officially recognized group focusing on the Asian-American ethnicity. But in most cases, the forging of Asian-American group identity happens on non-conscious or subconscious levels.

The formation of "friendships" focusing on Asian-Americans attests to a subconscious search for meaning and identity on group levels. Of course, the process is a part of the rejection they have experienced by whites, blacks, and Hispanics who may form dominant or significant sub-dominant groups in the high school. In a sense, the American high school can be seen as the place where group identity experiments happen by the initiation of the subjects of that experiment. Unfortunately, much of the study of American ethnic identity has ignored the process of group identity formation at the high school level. It is understandable why such a study is difficult. There are too many variables. High schools are vastly different based on the geographical location. Taking African-Americans as a group, we can even illustrate our point. Just because one area is black does not mean it is the same. There are regions where there is a heavy concentration of Caribbean Americans. So, for example, one school may have a dominant black population, but most of them are Caribbean. Their historical experience and identity markers may vary significantly from African-American identity markers stemming from the days of slavery and the days of the civil rights movement. How would a sociologist and psychologist account for this?

More importantly, the sociologist can spend 5 years observing this predominantly Caribbean high school to understand the characteristics of group identity in that high school and make some scientific evaluations. But who is to say that the scientific analysis in that high school holds true for a high school a mile or two away where the predominant black population is African-American and not Caribbean American. Their identity markers are completely different as are their oral histories and communal experiences. Thus, the scientific analysis is useless and is only particular to that one high school with predominantly Caribbean population. Of course, one can say that at least that scientific study may be useful for analyzing other high schools dominated by Caribbean Americans. This can be true. But at the formative stage of high school development, one cannot discount regional influences. Thus, a Caribbean American growing up in New Jersey will be completely different from a Caribbean American growing up in California. Because high school is where identity is formed, regionalism will impact that identity more than time in college or the workplace. But most importantly, it is important to be aware that high school is a period of experimentation in terms of identity. They may not be sure who they are individually or as a member of a particular group. They are searching for some identity. The process of identity searching becomes more normalized or stabilized as an adult. This is why sociologists and psychologists have refrained from extensive analysis of ethnic high school identity. Those who have engaged in such so-called scientific study of youth and ethnicity among youth have often failed.

Certainly, a white researcher studying Hispanic youths have no idea where to start. They cannot even understand Hispanic adults, so how will they understand Hispanic children and youth? Furthermore, for scientific study to work, the youth will have to answer the questions of the researcher. Most Hispanics will be inhibited from answering the questions honestly when asked by whites or people who are not perceived as a part of their identity group. This is natural. Identity formation is a complex process and it is most complex during teenage years. Of course, the white researcher cannot accuse Hispanic youth of lying or bearing false testimony. It is possible that the teenager may waver from one identity position to another and give a "truthful" answer at a particular time. The Hispanic youth's identity is not yet fixed at the point of high school. It is a period of experimentation in terms of identity. Even if the Hispanic youth lied, the sociologist cannot fault the teenager for wanting to protect his own group identity and individual identity tied to his Hispanic group identity. This may happen among adult subject, but it should most certainly be expected among teenagers. The white sociologist must acknowledge that the Hispanic youth's identity on individual and group levels is formed by the process of rejection by whites, most likely. So, why should the Hispanic youth trust the white sociologist? Is he not a part of the problem of rejection by white students in his high school? Such rationale runs through the minds of Asian-American youths as well. Why should a Chinese-American youth trust a white Jewish American sociologist when she tells him that she wants the best for him and wants to conduct an objective study of Chinese-Americans? The Chinese-American youth's mistrust of his white high school mates will filter into his mistrust of the white sociologist. It is nearly impossible for ethnically white Jewish sociologist to conduct an objective study of Asian-American high school student group identity because she is not Asian-American.

Besides the problem attached to being able to get accurate data from the Asian-American teenagers, the white Jewish sociologist has to recognize that she comes with biases as a white Jewish woman. Foucault and Post-modernism has shown that there is no objectivity in the world. All data is fundamentally skewed because the scientist comes with her biases. So, the white Jewish sociologists will start with her set of prejudices about Asian-Americans and about sociology and how the so-called scientific analysis should be conducted. The plethora of variables which skews her so-called scientific analysis makes it nearly impossible for her to make an accurate assessment of her Asian-American subjects even if they provide her with completely honest data. Her systematization of the data, analysis of the data, and conclusions regarding the so-called data will be inaccurate. The reason that ethnic problems are exponentially growing in America is that many whites – such as our example of white Jewish sociologists – have far too long conducted ethnic studies and given their white-biased conclusions, which are far from accuracy. Their biased conclusions provided no real helpful data for the well functioning of the society. Best sociological analysis of ethnic groups can only be conducted by the members of that group. Harvard education cannot provide freedom from inborn (and "learned" in the context of the in-group) biases from being a white Jewish sociologist. She is white more than she is a sociologist. She is existentially white, whereas she conducts sociology as a job based on a set of propositions that she has decided to accept and a set of propositions that she had decided to reject. For instance, you can be a follower of Freedman or a follower of Keynes in economics, but you cannot be both because their ideas are fundamentally opposed. In other words, you can be a follower of Hillel or a follower of Shammai, but as a religious Jew, you cannot be a follower of both because they have fundamentally opposing ways of interpreting the Jewish Law in many cases. The white Jewish sociologist has chosen which of the influential sociologists she will follow and that will color her work. She can choose a theory but she cannot choose not to be white. It is an existential fact that she is white. Thus, she cannot make an accurate reading of Asian ethnicity that is in transition at the current moment, even if she has a set of accurate theories. Her very existence as a white person will anchor the supposedly accurate theory on a shaky foundation. Besides, how many Asian Jews are there in the world? There may be a Korean adopted by Jews who was raised Jewish, or a Korean who converts to Judaism because she married a Jewish man, but Asian Jews are hard to find. Thus, the white Jewish sociologist's predominant religious identity will skew her analysis of Asians who have never come into contact with Judaism in any significant way. Therefore, it is impossible for a white Jewish woman to make an accurate reading of Asian-American youths. Her sociology analysis may get her tenure at Yale University but it is not accurate in any real way. This is the reason why America's ethnic problems are being compounded. White experts are making the situation worse because not only is it that not a single white ethnic studies expert can make even a closely accurate assessment of Asian-Americans through her research, her so-called scientific research used to frame America's governmental and social policies for Asian-Americans will compound the already existent problems because there will be more of her existentially white identity and her Jewish religious perspectives imbedded in her so-called scientific analysis.

In contrast to America's error of using white ethnic studies experts, Europe has been generally good in using ethnic experts to conduct research into their ethnic groups. This reduces the margin of error. The fact that white professors at Harvard University teach courses on Asian-American ethnic identity shows to what extent the legacy of slavery and segregation have impacted America's elite institutions. If the research had no relevance for society, it may be amusing. But since the US government and various social agencies use research by these white analysts who have no real clue to the realities of Asian-American ethnicity, US government consistently gets it wrong. This is clearly evident in the plight of ethnic relations facing America, today. The white Jewish female sociologist is to blame because no matter how she tries, she cannot understand Asian-American group identity accurately. If one asked her, the white Jewish female sociologist will be the first one to tell you that it is impossible for an Asian-American man to understand modern American Jewish ethnicity "really." Although she may balk at an Asian-American analysis of the modern Jewish woman, she herself will feel no remorse or hesitation about making conclusions about Asian-Americans in ethnic studies courses at the University of Pennsylvania.

In fact, many Jewish studies programs in America's secular universities will not hire someone who is not Jewish as a professor. There is a fundamentalist assumption in the Jewish world that Jewish studies must be done by Jews because Gentiles do not really understand the Jewish Question or the Jewish "predicament." This perspective has been expounded in many publications by Jewish studies experts who are themselves Jewish – whether religious or "secular." They understand inherently that there are biases that can skew information gathering and information analysis. Members of Jewish studies programs in the United States may emphasize that they minimize the error in understanding modern Jewish identity due to the existential and metaphysical identity of the scholar being Jewish – various Jewish groups, such as the World Zionist Organization and the American Jewish Congress, in the United States emphasize that point as well. Surprisingly enough, many of these same Jewish professors assume that this principle does not hold in research into other group identities. For instance, when there is an ethnic studies course on Asian-Americans, some Jewish professors feel that they do not need Asian-American experts to teach such ethnic studies courses. Many students in the Ivy League have particularly complained about the "lily white" washing of ethnic studies courses. By this they mean that there is a fundamental white perspective (whether Jewish, atheist, or Christian) that is colonizing the study of Asians in America. Not only is there room for much error in understanding of the subjects involved, there is a perceived possibility of white efforts to colonize the people of color through academic research and teaching. Many Asians find it disturbing that white Jews have a double-standard in the quest for ethnic understanding and desire that white Jews apply same principles to Asian-American ethnic studies as they do to Jewish studies. Other white ethnic groups, such as the white Irish and white Scandinavians, have not fallen into the error of white Jewish scholars in this regard.

Of course, the error of white sociologists and errant white-dominated ethnic studies academic discipline do not directly impact Asian-American search for individual and group identity on the high school level. What they experience is the real world. What the white academics publish and write for policy makers is the fictive parallel universe that may capture a small part of the reality of Asian-American youth and their experience. Most Asian-American youths will never read a single book of sociology or ethnic studies during their high school years. Many may not read a single book of such kind in college if they are, for instance, biology and chemistry majors and shy away from ethnic studies courses because they are taught by white professors. Of course, this does not mean that they are not active participants in ethnic formation and identity. In fact, it is the ethnic studies professors at Harvard and Yale who are crossing their fingers to get things right vis-à-vis Asian-Americans whom they are studying. Asian-American high school students and college students are, by their existential and metaphysical realities intrinsic to them, formers, shapers, and guiders of the ethnic identity and individual identity tied to their ethnic being, whether they are aware of their participation in the process or not.

Search for meaning and identity on the individual level and the group level is certainly a part of the everyday experience of Korean-Americans, particularly in high school and college. The fact is that Korean-American students experience social rejection on all kinds of levels for being a people of color. However, they do not always understand the nature of their rejection. Many may think that they are being rejected on account of something that is particular to them. This, of course, can be the case. But more often than not, their identity as Korean-Americans is fundamentally a constitutive part of the rationale for rejection by others. It can, in fact, be a combination of their personal individual traits and the reality of their visible Koreanness. It is hard to mistake a Korean when one sees him. One may not think that he is a Korean per see, but one will know after one second of looking that he is not white. He is an Asian. Despite the fact that Koreanness is the most visible trait of any Korean-American individual, Korean-American high school students and college students often do not consider the role that this plays in his rejection.

There are several reasons why the visible Korean identity is ignored by Korean-American high school students and college students. First of all, it is painful to think about the Korean identity. Korean-American high school students and college students are aware that they are Korean-Americans. They know that they are visibly different from dominant peoples. They understand further that their Korean traits are something they cannot change; this is certainly the case with physical attributes. Thus, they know they can better themselves athletically by joining the football team and the track team, but they know that no matter how good they are in football and in track, they still will be visibly Korean. Thus, when a Korean-American walks in the streets of his neighborhood where he led his football team to a national championship as the football captain of his large public high school, he will still often be mistaken for a Korean who just immigrated to the United States from Korea or some other Asian country. White Americans cannot tell the difference between a FOB ("Fresh off the Boat") Korean and a Banana (completely assimilated) Korean. They are visibly Korean. Because Korean-American high school students and college students understand that the visible Korean identity is something they cannot change while they can change other attributes – such as academics and athletics – they prefer to ignore it in computing their own personal identity, especially when a rejection by the larger group is involved. If the larger group rejects a person because he is not as good of a track player, he can practice and become the best track player on the team. If the larger group rejects a person because his football skills are below par, then he can run the exercises and become the best in his team. If he is rejected because his academic qualification is not good enough, he can always work harder to advance your academic skills to be among the best. But there is nothing to do to change his visible Korean identity. He will look Korean no matter what he does. It is one area where he has absolutely no control. Thus, psychologically it is easier just to push this constant out of his mind and focus on the variables that can be controlled. And that is what Korean-American youth do.

   Korean-American youth do not want to think about their Korean identity or talk about it among their peer groups or even with their parents. Most Korean-American youth will tell you that even if they have the best relationship with their parents, they have never talked about the implications of their Korean identity in the

American context in any serious conversation with them. The topic is shunned and ignored. Of course, ignoring the problem does not mean that it does not exist. In fact, the Korean identity is the most significant identity marker for most Korean-American high school students and college students. It trumps all other identities, such as being an excellent athlete or a great student. Simply put, when anyone sees a Korean-American, they will know that he is a Korean or some kind of an Asian. That is the first impression even before he opens his mouth. In America, there is a saying: "First impression is everything." For all Korean-Americans, the first impression is that he is visibly Korean. Every other impression he makes after this initial impression is built on the fact of *that* first impression. The fact of his visible Koreanness colors all of his other achievements. Thus, his Koreanness is something he cannot ignore.

What is the Korean-American to do? Korean-American high school students and college students should invest time and energy to understand the fact of their Korean-American identity and the impact it can have on their life. If a Korean-American does not understand or think about the implications of his Korean identity, then he will always remain an ignorant and haplessly oblivious victim of that first impression or that primary identity marker. But if a Korean-American understands the fact and the implications of his visible Korean identity, he can modify the variables that he can control to defend the potential threats that may arise because of the constant in his identity, which is the visible Koreanness. Ignorance is not bliss in this case because whether he is ignorant or not, his visible Koreanness will impact him and his future. All around him see that he is visibly Korean, whether he wants to ignore this main aspect of himself or not. It can be likened to gravity. No matter how much a person wants to deny the reality of gravity, he is bound by it. He could say, "I don't believe in gravity. Gravity does not exist." He could say this to all he wants and to everyone he meets. He could say it to himself everyday when he gets up in the morning. It does not change the fact.

Gravity exists and one is a "victim" of gravity on a daily level. There is no day when gravity does not impact his existence. Being Korean-American in the United States is similar. He could tell himself everyday that the visible Asianness does not exist or does not matter. He could say that others will not notice it and say this until he is blue in the face. That does not matter. He is visibly different. He is a Korean-American with visible Korean attributes. And that visible difference will have some bearing every day.

Unfortunately, however, at this point in Korean-American history, there is almost no discourse on Korean-American identity in the home, school, church, and other Korean-American social associations. It is understandable to a certain extent why this can be the case on the group level. Parents of Korean-American youth tend to be immigrants from Korea who were not born in the United States. Their primary cultural and social reference points are Korean. Many even work primarily with Koreans and have primarily Korean friends, whom they have known for decades. For many of the parents of Korean-American high school students and college students, visible Korean identity does not hurt them in their work or social life. They encounter mostly Koreans in their work setting – as colleagues and bosses. They fraternize mostly with Koreans after work in their free time. The Korean-American question based on visible Korean identity may not be as pressing for them as it is for their children who have predominantly non-Korean social associations and have to subjugate themselves even in the microcosm of the classroom to a predominantly non-Korean populace. Thus, it is understandable why parents of Korean-American teenagers and college students almost never ask them about their Korean identity and their identity quest. They merely assume that they are secure the way they are. Furthermore, most parents of Korean-American youth rarely struggle with Korean identity. They know they are Koreans and they are secure and happy in that identity. Of course, for Korean-American teens and college students, this is not the case. Like all teenagers, they are in search of identity. This is a natural part of being teenagers. But unlike the teenagers of dominant groups, Korean-American youth and college students have to struggle with their visible difference (from dominant white, black, and Hispanic groups).

For the same reason that parents rarely discuss Korean identity and its implications with their Korean-American teens and college students, Korean-American churches rarely discuss the fact and meaning of Korean identity. Thus, most Korean-American teens and college students have never discussed in their youth groups or college groups what it means to be Korean-American in modern-day America. The fact is, like their parents, the leadership in Korean-American churches tend to be largely immigrants from Korea who have their primary identity in the Old Country. Many of them associate mostly with Koreans in the work place and in social outings. Many of them never have to think about the struggles of Korean-American teenagers and college students in the larger American context or even in the microcosm of the classroom – for instance, with some 25 students, who are mostly not Korean-Americans. Thus, Korean-American youth and college students are left to negotiate their identity without much guidance or direction.

Thus, many Korean-American teenagers and college students struggle as they attempt to find meaning and identity on individual and group levels. This process is not necessarily done on a conscious level, particularly at the high school level. This explains why many Korean-American high school students find a type of subgroup identity within the mainstream flow of their high schools in small friendship groups that tend to be predominantly Asian-American. To a large extent, Chinese-Americans as well as other Asian-American students experience similar trends of rejection as Korean-Americans. Thus, it is not surprising that Korean-Americans gravitate toward other Asian-Americans, who also feel kinship with Korean-Americans. In fact, when looking in from the outside, it will be impossible to tell a visible difference among Korean-Americans, Chinese-Americans, and Japanese-Americans. They all look alike, literally. Since they are born in the United

States, many of them cannot speak the language of their ancestry fluently. And those who can speak the language fluently often do not speak the language in the context of their high school. Most often, they will not find others in their ethnic group who can speak the language as well. More often, they will be a part of the larger Asian-American friendship group, rather than have a collection of friends who are Korean-Americans. Thus, Korean-Americans will feel awkward speaking Korean when there are Chinese-Americans and Japanese-Americans in their Asian-American friendship group. The case will be similar for Chinese-Americans and Japanese-Americans in the friendship group.

In a sense, therefore, the group identity that Korean-American high school students have negotiated for themselves can be seen as a pan-Asian-American identity and not a distinctively Korean-American identity. This may seem like a practical solution for many Korean-American high school students born in the United States. First of all, they are not strongly tied to their Korean roots. Many Korean-American teenagers cannot speak Korean well, if at all. Many Korean-Americans do not like Korean food like their parents, and some may be able to live without Korean food, which would be impossible for their immigrant parents. Even in terms of cultural practices, Korean-American teenagers do not behave in Korean ways. Most often, they relate in cultural ways reminiscent of the general American culture. This is understandable since they have been brought up in the United States and educated in the American school system. Their teachers will perpetuate a general American culture and values that may be a part of the "American" life. Of course, many of these cultural traits may be taken up on superficial levels, but in terms of function, they play a visible role in the lives of Korean-American teens. Besides cultural proximity to America more than Korea, Korean-American teens have no sense of real closeness to Korea. Many Korean-American teens have never been to Korea, ever, and many do not have any real interest in visiting. They are happy in America and they expect to live the rest of their lives in America. In fact, many

Korean-Americans share the patriotic American sentiment that those who refuse to learn English should "go back to where they came from." Korean-American teens are fluent in English and often are at the top of their classes in high school. For them, they instinctively believe that living in America requires learning English and manoeuvring the American system as a participant in the system. Even if they are not fully accepted in the American society due to their visible Koreanness, they consider American culture as their own and have expectations of others to abide by their "culture." In a sense, therefore, we can speak of Korean-Americans having a type of pride in their American roots.

But looked at it from another angle, they can be said to have no other choice. Some Korean-Americans are born in the United States, and Korean culture often confuses them. They feel that they understand American culture best and they have, at least on a superficial level, adopted it (whether consciously or subconsciously) as their own culture. Thus, in comments Korean-Americans make about the English language – such as, "those who do not want to learn the English language should go back to where they came from" – they betray their own cultural value. Of course, most Korean-Americans who say this are not talking about Korean immigrants (at least consciously). They are talking about Mexican immigrants or immigrants from other countries, besides Korea. This should not be surprising because Korean-Americans are trying to negotiate their identity between the American culture which they feel comfortable with and the Korean culture which they do not understand. If it were not for their visible Koreanness, many of the Korean-American teenagers will be happy to renounce their Korean identity and exist as "Americans." But as it is, this is impossible. They look visibly Asian and will remain so until the time of their death. Their visible Koreanness will impede their professional advancement and hinder their full acceptance into dominant social structures. Thus, as much as they may want, they cannot succeed in shedding the Korean past. Thus, the Dean of Yale Law School may be Korean-American, named Harold Koh. He is even married to a white woman. But most do not see him as "American." In common popular conversations, people refer to that "Korean Dean" of Yale Law School. No matter how often Professor Koh may protest, he cannot not rid himself of his visible Koreanness. The case is the same for all Korean-American teens in American high schools, today. They will always be "Korean" or "Asian" because of their visible Koreanness.

Thus, it is quite easy to see why Korean-Americans gravitate toward those who share their experiences and have the same appearance as they. Language is no barrier among Korean-American teens, Chinese-American high school students, and Japanese-American youth, so they could become friend across ethnic lines within the Asian-American group identity. In this regard, they are completely different from their parents. You will be hard-pressed to find Korean-American parents who have Chinese-American friends or Japanese-American friends. Their social group is often almost exclusively Korean. This is the case with Chinese-Americans and Japanese-Americans as well. Immigrants tend to stick to members of the Old Country. The children of the immigrants are completely different, of course. And Korean-American teens find their group identity with other Asian-Americans. Thus, when asked about their identity, most Korean-Americans will prefer to say "Asian" or "Asian-American" rather than "Korean" or "Korean-American." They may humor their parents and other members of the Korean in-group by saying that they are "Korean." But certainly in the larger context of the American society, most Korean-American teens of today tend to use a broader "Asian" or "Asian-American" self-designation.

Such effort to use pan-Asian identity marker can be seen as a survival mechanism. Whether they recognize consciously or not, these Korean-American teens are negotiating their survivability within the dominant American society. There are simply not many Korean-Americans in their high schools. When they say "Korean" or "Korean-American," they may feel that they are distancing themselves from Chinese-Americans and Japanese-Americans.

And in actuality, it may be possible that their Chinese-American and Japanese-American friends may take offense at their specific self-delineation of "Korean-American." If they do take offense, then they may be hesitant to be there as a friend or in defense when help is needed. Consciously or unconsciously, Korean-American teens have developed a coping mechanism to survive the difficulties of high school life, where group identity matters far more than in college – particularly, on a daily basis.

Furthermore, Korean-American teens have developed greater sensitivity to ethnic discourse than their parents. And it is this identity discourse sensitivity that makes them use a pan-Asian identity marker rather than a specific Korean identity marker. Thus, Korean-American teens are genuinely worried about offending the sensitivities of Chinese-Americans and Japanese-Americans. They would prefer that word does not travel back to their non-Korean Asian-American friends that they have in a sense segregated themselves from the pan-Asian friendship group. Such concern would have been non-existent a decade ago, but a combination of factors changed that. First of all, in the past most Korean-Americans, Chinese-Americans, and Japanese-Americans functioned with a strong pride for their ethnic identity attached to their Old Country. They took pride in themselves and were not offended by other Asian-Americans taking pride in their particular ethnic identity. But things have changed. A pan-Asian-American identity has been created on college campuses and by Asian-American intellectuals. Now, we are beginning to see the fruits of the efforts of the past two decades to forge an Asian-American identity. The new generation of Korean-Americans fully subscribe to the vision. Secondly, the last generation of Korean-Americans had mostly immigrant leaders in the Korean-American community who came to America as grown adults. These leaders had most of their upbringing in Korea. Now, the situation is different. The majority of Korean-American leaders – particularly those who lead youth groups and other types of Korean-American youth associations – went through the American educational system and spent much of their childhood in the United States, even if they may have been born in Korea. And more and more, Korean-American leaders of youth are American-born Koreans. For these new leaders, Korean identity may not seem as important as an Asian identity. When these Korean-Americans were in college, many of them participated in pan-Asian events. So, they may fundamentally believe in a pan-Asian identity over and against distinctively Korean-centric identity. It is understandable that Korean-American youth learning from Korean-American leaders of this persuasion will tend toward the pan-Asian direction over and against the distinctively Korean-centric direction preferred by their parents. Thus, Korean-American teens of today not only learn sensitivity toward pan-Asian discourse in the context of the group identity they are trying to negotiate in their high schools; they also formalize the process in the context of their Korean-American church youth groups under Korean-American leaders of such a persuasion.

For many Korean-American teens, sensitivity toward pan-Asian identity has become an integral part of their worldview and identity that even when they talk among Koreans, they would refer to themselves as "Asians" or "Asian-Americans" rather than "Korean" or "Korean-American." Many Korean-American parents find this disturbing, since they generally do not see Chinse-Americans and Japanese-Americans as a part of their group. This would be the case for parents of Chinse-American and Japanese-American teens as well. There is an absence of strong Asian-American identity and friendship in the generation of the parents of Korean-American teens of today. The Korean-American parents are generally 10-20 years older than current Korean-American church youth group leaders who are 5-10 years older than their children. Korean-American parents are often shocked to find that their children think that there is no problem marrying Chinese-Americans and Japanese-Americans. The Korean-American youth often describe marrying Chinese-Americans and Japanese-Americans as same as marrying Korean-Americans. This is understandable because they have negotiated their group identity as "Asian" or "Asian-American" rather than "Korean" or "Korean-American" in their high school context. And the Korean-American teens are often surprised to find that their parents prefer them to marry whites rather than Chinese-Americans and Japanese-Americans.

For most Korean-American parents, not marrying Koreans is bad. Marrying people who look like Koreans does not compensate. This is understandable in light of the fact that Korean-American parents have a strong Koran-centric identity. Koreans in Korea have strong attitudes toward China and Japan in the same way that the French dislike Germans and the English hate the French. They all look similar and they have more or less similar culture and shared history, although they have different languages. In the same way, China, Korea, and Japan share similarities in culture (although there are some noticeable differences!) and look similar although their languages differ. Koreans from Korea do not particularly like the Chinese or the Japanese in the same way the French do not particularly like the English and Germans. In fact, the French may prefer their children to marry Canadians rather than marry English or Germans. In the same way, Koreans prefer that their children marry white Americans rather than the Chinese or the Japanese. The conflicts of the Old Country have a bearing in the New Country and in the value system of the immigrants to the New Country. Their children cannot understand this because they do not have Korea as their central reference point. Their central reference point is America and within the dominant culture they have negotiated an Asian-American identity. The perspective, therefore, is fundamentally different between Korean-American teens and their parents when it comes to marrying Chinese or Japanese. Both Korean-American teens and their parents are in for a rude awakening in this regard because the trend of Korean-Americans marrying Chinese-Americans or other Asian-Americans is growing at an exponential rate, currently. The rate of marrying white-Americans is growing but not to the same extent.

This can be understandable in light of the fact that the negotiated Asian-American identity continues to play a significant role in college. And in college, many can meet their love and marry them.

What actually happens in college in terms of group identity negotiation for Korean-Americans? This merits a closer examination because there is a shift in Asian-American identity dynamics on the college level that does not exist or is minimal at the high school level. This may be due to the fact that high schools often have American-born Asian-Americans but colleges often have a significant Asian international student population. In fact, in some colleges, the number of Koreans who spent at least half of their life in Korea equals the number of Korean-American students born in the United States. There are Koreans who finished their high school education in Korea who come to America to study for their bachelor's degree. There are Koreans who studied a part of their college program in Korea who transfer to American universities. There are Koreans who have a bachelor's degree in Korea who decide to take a second bachelor's degree in the United States. There are some Koreans who went to international schools around the world whose parents live in Korea, and they decide to pursue their college degree in the USA. There are those who came to the United States for a part of their high school education who go to college in the United States. The number of this group has been increasing steadily for the past 10 years. In fact, in some Korean-American churches, one will find that over 30 per cent of the youth group will comprise high school students of this type. They often come only with their mother to live in the United States and they are here only to pursue their high school education and higher education. The father remains in Korea and works there to send financial support for his children living with their mother and studying in the USA. In certain cases, the parents of Korean high school students both live in Korea, and the children live with a Korean host family introduced by Korean churches. Such a reality makes American colleges very interesting places for Korean-Americans.

So, what happens in America's colleges as the result of such a complex reality facing Korean-Americans? There are two strong trends for Korean-Americans. One trend is for Korean-Americans to continue in the trend set in high school; they will continue to forge a strong Asian-American identity over and against a distinctive Korean identity. The other trend is for Korean-Americans to develop a strong Korea-centric identity.

The first trend seems "normal." If Korean-American teens have been pursuing a negotiated Asian-American identity, then it is logical for them to continue to pursue the identity in which they have invested time and energy. Furthermore, they have developed strong friends in a wider pan-Asian-American identity group, and it is possible that they can go to the same college together, especially to state universities. Furthermore, Korean-American teens who have been comfortable in a pan-Asian-American friendship group have developed a type of familiarity with other Asian-Americans and may feel comfortable in such a permutation. They may be used to not talking distinctively about Korean issues or talking in the Korean language. They may have developed a value system that privileges a pan-Asian identity over against a distinctively Korean-American identity. Even though they may have been adolescents in high school, by the time that they reach college, they would have developed some core values for themselves relating to their identity. While some may still be in the "search and find" mode of identity discovery, other Korean-Americans may feel that they understand their individual and group identity in terms of the vested pan-Asian-American identity. These Korean-Americans will joyfully or even purposefully pursue Asian-American friendship groups over and against distinctively Korean-American friendship groups. It is not uncommon to find Korean-Americans who do not like to be among just Korean-Americans. They prefer to be near a more diverse Asian-American population that includes Chinese-Americans and Japanese-Americans.

It is possible to question whether their preference for an Asian-American identity at the college level is a form of rejection of the self and a compromised group identity resulting from their experience of rejection by the dominant groups. In other words, some Korean-Americans did not want to be with Asian-Americans predominantly but because of the flow of dominant culture which actively or passively excluded them, they were resigned to the second best thing, so to speak. Their group identity was not a part of the dominant group identity, but on the other hand it was not a "retreat" into Korean identity either.

Some Korean-Americans may feel that having all Korean friends signals a defeat. They could not "hack" it in the dominant group, so they were running back to their ethnic group with their tail between their legs. They did not want to be in a situation where they had to admit to themselves that they could not hack it in America as Americans. They may prefer to be Bananas but if they could not be Bananas because of the rejection by the dominant group, they were still going to fight on and become as much a part of the wider American culture as possible. In a sense, therefore, they are driven by their psychological need for acceptance and a sense of ideological devotion to a concept of diversity in America. There are not a few Korean-Americans who fall into this group.

Of course, it is possible that some Korean-Americans hate their Korean identity, for whatever reason. It is possible to talk about self hatred for some Korean-Americans. It may be due to the fact that some Korean-Americans had a bad experience in Korean cultural contexts. Maybe they were poked fun of by Koreans because they could not speak Korean. Maybe they could not act according to Korean cultural mores and they encountered rejection as a result. It is possible that they just hate things Korean because they "hate" their parents, for whatever reason. Many teenagers hate their parents but in the case of Korean-American teens, this can take on ethic overtones. Thus, a Korean-American teen who hates his parents may feel that rejecting of Korean identity allows him to express his deep seated hatred of his parents. For him, this is seen as a form of self-empowerment. It may appear to be self hatred by other Korean-Americans, but it is a way that he feels he is taking control of his own life which he feels he needs as an adult in college. In such cases, the Korean-American individual will most likely say "goodbye" to his parents, and his parents may regret to their dying days the fact that they did not adequately inculcate a Korean-centric identity for their son. For many Korean-Americans, rejection of Korean culture and identity can coincide with or even precede rejection of their parents as individuals. In other words, rejecting Koreanness can be a harbinger of their disowning of their parents.

Korean-American college students in this group often join pan-Asian groups and are activists for pan-Asian causes. There are groups such as Asian-American Students Associations or the Pan-Asian Council. Korean-Americans who opt for a pan-Asian friendship group and identity will be active within the politically and socially delineated agenda set by this group. It is interesting to note that most Koreans who are very active in Asian-American groups tend to shy away from distinctively Korean-American groups and friendship groups. Some may feel that those who would be concerned about Asian-American empowerment will care about the good of their particular Asian-American community (namely, Korean-American), but his is not always the case. There are several reasons for this.

Goals of Asian-American groups often come in direct conflict with Korean-American student associations. For instance, most Asian-Americans are not Christians. Many Chinese-Americans tend to be Buddhists and many Japanese-Americans tend to be Shintoists or atheists. Korean-Americans, on the other hand, tend to be evangelical Christians. Many of them tend to be Fundamentalist Christians of the Southern Baptist kind. Thus, when many Asian-American groups join campus-wide movements to support homosexuality and abortion – typically liberal agendas – Korean-American groups tend to shy away from it or even oppose it. There are more Korean-American Bible study groups than there are Korean-American social associations at any given American university. Certainly, this is not the case for the Chinese-American community and the Japanese-American community. This is not the case for the Filipino community or any other Asian-American community, besides the Korean-American community. Thus, being a strong part of the Asian-American movement in the United States necessarily will mean setting oneself apart from the Korean-American community. For some reason, Asian-American groups and their agendas have been strongly leftist and even bordering on a type of social communism, at least historically. This trend may change in the future, but at this point in American history, it does seem like the change is nowhere in the near future.

There are other reasons why Korean-Americans who participate in Asian-American groups and movements tend to set themselves apart from Korean-Americans. In terms of dating, even, Korean-Americans in Asian-American groups will date Chinese-Americans or Filipino-Americans. This would not be welcomed by members of Korean-American student organizations. This is not surprising since Korean-American student organizations exist to celebrate Koreanness. For many members, it is an opportunity to discover the inner Korean within, so to speak. Korean-American student groups often encourage activities that help advance awareness of the Korean identity and Korean-centric loyalties. For instance, Korean-American student groups will sponsor Korean movie nights. For many Korean-American college students born in America, this will be their first exposure to Korean movies (although they will have to read the subtitles since they cannot understand Korean). Furthermore, Korean-Americans in Korean-American student groups will encourage Korean identity through Korean dating. Thus, Korean-American student associations will sponsor Korean parties for Koreans to meet each other and even find a future mate to form a nice Korean-American family with. Thus, they may balk at Korean-Americans who date Chinese or Japanese. Korean-Americans who participate in pan-Asian activities will sense a type of rejection of them and their significant other and this will fuel their dislike of things Korean.

While there is a significant number of Korean-Americans who opt for the pan-Asian-American group identity as over against the distinctively Korean-American group identity, there are many who throw in their hat with those who try to forge a distinctively Korean-American ethnic identity and Korean-American group associations. Even among those who had participated in predominantly Asian-American friendship group in high school, there may be those who would prefer to explore a more distinctively Korean-American identity in college. Maybe they had Chinese-American and Japanese-American friends in high school because there were not many Korean-Americans. But now that they are in college, they do not have that problem. There are many Korean-Americans. And unlike high school, there are Korean-American associations that they can easily join. Thus, some Korean-Americans abandon their previous choice of pan-Asian-American group identity for a more distinctively Korean-American identity.

For other Korean-Americans, they find that the Korean-American group association provides a type of Linus's safety blanket. They find that many Korean-Americans in this group have experienced similar experiences to their own. They have Korean parents who emphasize Korean culture. Like them, they rebelled a bit against that. But like them, they have an interest in Korean culture and a desire to explore Korean identity. A grouping of kindred spirits was exactly what they were looking for. They feel safe and comfortable in such an empathetic setting. Furthermore, these Korean-Americans feel that they feel like being at home. They may have complained about their Korean parents, but they actually liked more than not about what made them who they are – of course, Koreanness is a large part of that. While being away from home, Korean-American youth feel homesick and crave the kind of environment that their family provided. Korean-American student association may be the closest thing to their home. Some of the Korean-Americans in Korean-American student associations may even remind them of their younger brother they miss, for instance.

Besides Korean-Americans who see Korean-American student groups as a type of Linus's blanket, there are other Korean-Americans who are more ideologically driven. In other words, some Korean-American college students believe that a distinctively Korean-centric identity group is a value in and of itself. They can come to this conclusion via different routes, of course. It is possible that they were a part of a rare lot in high school who emphasized distinctive Korean identity. Maybe they resented Japanese-Americans because of the history of Japan occupying Korea for 35 years (1910-1945). Maybe they shied away from friendships with Chinese-Americans because they had a grandfather who was shot dead during the Korean War in Seoul by the invading Chinese Red Army soldiers who supported the Communist North Korea. It is possible that some of these Korean-Americans were among those who tried to emphasize the beauty of Korean history and culture to their predominantly white friends in a high school which did not have many Korean students. Thus, it is possible that some Korean-American college students are just continuing their ideological position that they had in high school.

Other Korean-Americans may have come to this position through a different route. Maybe they were Bananas in high school. They rejected Korean culture and had exclusively white friends. But when they entered college, they had a type of personal epiphany. They thus came to swing in the completely opposite direction from their Banana days and became aggressively Korean-centric. These group of Koreans most likely will be more fervent than those Korean-Americans who were always quite Korean-centric. It is the zeal of a new convert to a new religion. They may feel that they have a vested interest in proving to themselves and to others that they are truly "born-again" to a Korean-centric vision of life. There is not a few in this group of Korean-Americans because there are a lot of Korean-Americans still who attend high schools where there are negligible number of Korean-Americans or Asian-Americans, for that matter.

Besides the ideologically driven Korean-Americans who glue themselves to Korean-American groups, there are those who actively participate in Korean-American groups because they are international students from Korea. There is a sizable number of international students who neither hold a Green Card or the American citizenship in many of America's universities. Obviously, they will not see themselves as Americans in any shape or form. They are Korean citizens. They hold an international student visa. They are loyal to Korea and are legally subjects of that nation. These Koreans will attend Korean-American student groups because they are generally the only Korean student groups on campus. Unlike Korean-Americans, these Koreans do not struggle with their identity. They see themselves as Korean and will have predominantly Korean-speaking friends. They will share the attitudes of Koreans in Korea. And they will probably listen to more Korean music than American music. Their email address will have "kr" (for Korea) in the end, rather than "com" or "net." Their website home page will have Korean words. And their personal computer will have the XP Korean Home edition. All the pop-up notices will be in Korean and not in English. They participate in Korean-American student groups with neither delusions about nor quest for Korean identity. However, they play a central role in Korean-American student groups in directing them in a more powerfully Korean-centric direction.

Because Korean international students will always emphasize Korea and Korean issues within the Korean-American student associations, they will become conduits for Korean-American culture for Korean-Americans who are hazy about their Korean identity. In fact, many Korean-Americans searching for their Korean identity may find their presence very welcome because they have no other way to understand what Korean culture is if it were not for the strong presence of international students from Korea. Thus, it is not surprising that often Korean international students have dominant positions within Korean-American students' associations as leaders and key players. It is no accident that programs to relieve North Korean famine started to crop up like wildfire among America's universities. It was the fuel of immigrant students from Korea that inflamed Korean-American students' zeal for North Korean famine relief. Many Korean-Americans who could have cared less about North Korea suddenly came to devote hours and hours to North Korean famine relief. All major universities in America have some form of North Korean famine relief organization set up by students. The credit for such achievement must be given to international students from Korea in large part because they were often the initiators or fuelers of such movements. Korean-American students may give a lot of their time and energy to such efforts but it was not their idea initially, and the main leadership remains – to this day – in the hands of Korean international students and the main, central offices, in Korea.

It must not be forgotten that any Korean-centric identity will seek to establish a stronger bond with the Old Country. This is necessarily the case because there is really nothing in America that is distinctively Korean in character. Korean-American communities and churches all look to Korea for Korean-centric identity markers. Many Korean-Americans refuse to hire senior pastors from America because many Korean-Americans are disturbed by the "soft" position that many Korean clergy educated in America take in terms of Korean identity. For example, some Korean-Americans may not mind Koreans marrying non-Koreans. This is not the case with Koreans in Korea. The majority of Koreans still have serious problems with Koreans marrying non-Koreans. Functionally, of course, this is a serious taboo in Korea, although rhetoric may have become more politically correct in recent days. In fact, it is nearly impossible to function normally in the Korean community with a non-Korean spouse. There are exceptions, to be sure, but often these exceptions prove the rule. It is because many Korean-American parents do not want their children to marry whites or any other non-Koreans, that they desire inviting Korean clergy from Korea. Furthermore, many Koreans want to feel a connection to Korea. Thus, when they are ready to hire a senior pastor, they do not want to hire someone from America who may have forgotten what it was like being in Korea because he has lived in America over 20 years. Korean-Americans attend a Korean-American church for a reason. They are not at a white church or a black church because they want to experience Korean culture and community while worshipping their God. If they did not care about the Korean aspect, they would go to a good church nearby which was non-Korean, instead of driving some 40 minutes or more to attend a Korean-American church. Many of these Korean-American parents are also concerned that their children learn Korean ways and have Korean friends. If they did not go to a Korean-American church, some of their children may end up having no Korean friends. Thus, it is not surprising that Korean-Americans often look towards Korea for a fresh Korean to come and imbue their church with a Korean identity that will rub off on their children. In other words, it is consistent for a Korean-centric attitude to be coupled with a desire for a piece of the Old Country.

Such a trend characterizes Korean-American student groups. They are looking for a piece of Korea in their midst. Many Korean-American students who would like to go in a Korean-centric direction look towards Korea and students from Korea for direction. Thus, it is not surprising that many Koreans with a broken spoken English can play central roles in Korean-American student associations. In a sense, it may even be possible to say that many Korean-Americans who actively involve themselves in Korean-American student associations may have an inferiority complex toward international students from Korea. Some Korean-Americans join Korean-American student groups to get in touch with their Korean side, and these international students from Korea are fully in touch with their Korean-side. Thus, many Korean-American students look toward them for a type of leadership and feel a sense of inadequacy in regards to their own Koreanness (an integral part of their identity) that they want to have satisfied. Some Korean-Americans desire such security in their Korean identity.

Thus, Korean-American student associations have a different set of interests from pan-Asian-American student associations. Sometimes, the interests of Korean-American student groups come into conflict with pan-Asian-American student groups. It is, therefore, not surprising that Korean-Americans who are actively a part of Asian-American student groups can come into conflict with some of the members of Korean-American student associations. Such a conflict can exist at the college level, whereas they may be invisible in the high school level – particular colleges attract significant numbers of Asian students and these colleges have many Asian-American student groups, including those which are aggressively political tending toward the left. And it is generally in these colleges that there are many Korean-American students' groups which are aggressively seeking to define Korean identity.

Korean-American youth identity, whether at the high school level or at the college level, is a complex phenomenon. There is a search for identity and negotiation of various conflicting elements for a group identity. For many Korean-American teenagers, identity negotiation involves formation of Asian-American friendship groups that exist at the periphery of mainstream high school life. They functionally exist to support a group identity for individuals who have experienced rejection – whether active or passive – from the dominant population (white, black, or Hispanic). Often, the paucity of the number of Asians in a high school makes functional Asian friendship groups a necessity for teenage survival in the American high school system. In many cases, the necessity propelled group identity often becomes centralized as the search for identity by Korean-Americans (not only on the group identity level but on the individual identity level) takes a back seat. For some of them, this pan-Asian identity filters through their college experience and beyond. Some may even marry Asian-American who are not Korean-American or Korean.

The negotiation of identity is far more complex in college as the invasion of Korean-born, Korean-bred, and Korean-educated international students make their presence felt on the college scene.

They impede Korean-American student groups and make an indelible mark of influence. They add to the growing rift between Korean-American student groups and pan-Asian-American student groups, which become more and more America-centric in their concerns, purpose, and activities. The upshot of all the confusion is that there is a significant amount of uncertainty surrounding Korean-American identity on the college level. Perhaps, it may not be wrong to say that Korean-American college students are more confused about their identity than Korean-American high school students. There are just more variables to wade through. When many Korean-Americans graduate from college they are still in search of their identity. Many do not understand what Korean-American identity exactly is. And this creates a certain amount of instability for the Korean-American community at large and for Korean-American churches which seek to absorb them into their community. The future is yet to be written in terms of what direction Korean-American high students, college students, and recent college graduates will go. Right now, there is basically a big question mark.

Chapter 8:
"Korean-American Youth Dating and Marriage"

Integrally related to Korean-American search for group identity are the Korean-American dating scene and Korean-American marriage practices. It is generally understood in anthropology and sociology that marriage is a primary indicator of a society's value system and mores. There are several reasons why marriage plays such an integral role in society. Formation of the marriage bond is not a bonding merely of two individuals. It is nearly impossible to find a society where families of those who marry do not figure into the equation of marriage. This was the case in Europe throughout its history. In the Middle Ages, marriages were seen by wealthy families as a type of a business venture where two wealthy families bond through marriage to form a big wealth "conglomerate." Thus, as we have mergers and acquisitions based on the capitalist system today, in the Middle Ages there was the marriage to function as a type of a mergers and acquisitions system. Some claim that some European wealthy families still function with this antiquated notion of the marriage bond – even today. In the Middle Ages, even when wealth was not necessarily involved, marriage functioned as a type of a contract of the social kind. Thus, two families that did not get along or even have fought in the past would have the son of one family marry the daughter of the other family to ensure a type of peace between the two families. In such cases, it did not matter to the families involved whether the son and the daughter loved each other. However, what the two families were concerned about was the success of the marriage. They understood that the marriage was a type of a social contract, so if the marriage failed, they knew that the tenuous peace between the two formerly hostile families could come to an end. In fact, a failed marriage in this particular case may result in a worse situation than before the marriage contract was ratified in the bond of Holy Matrimony. Thus, both families worked to ensure that the husband and the wife would fulfil their marriage duties – including being faithful in marriage. Cheating could have dire consequences because the other party in the contract would bring grievances against the other party in the contract. In other words, if a husband cheated on his wife and the wife went back in tears to her parents regarding her husband's unfaithfulness, her parents can opt to restart hostilities against the family (and the extended group) of the husband. It is easy to understand that marriage was sacred on a social level. It may have been a sacrament in the Roman Catholic Church and was sacred in the church for that purpose, but in the context of the society, marriage was sacred because it was a social glue and one of the most serious types of social contracts. Thus, the church did not want divorce because they did not want a separation of what God has joined together in the bond of Holy Matrimony, but medieval society did not want divorce because it was the most serious breach of the social contract and a war (or other types of major social conflicts) could ensue as a result.

Like medieval Europe, Asia tended to view marriage as a type of social contract. Whether it is China or India, marriage has been seen as a type of social contract between families. In fact, for a large part of Asian history, marrying parties had no choice in the matter; they were to marry whom their parents have chosen for them. And their parents made a marriage partner choice based on concerns that their family faced. In many cases, marriage thus functioned as a type of social contract, not unlike in Europe. Two families that did not get along but wanted the two families to get along would contract their children for marriage, thereby securing "prosperity and peace" between the two families. And like in Europe, there were cases of marriages that functioned as an economic contract. Two wealthy families ensured a type of economic alliance by marrying the children of the two families to each other. The assumption was that the members of the two families would look out for the interests of each other and protect each other on the economic scene. Of course, it was assumed that there would be no backstabbing of any kind. Remarkably, therefore, the nature of marriage is quite similar between Europe and Asia throughout much of their history. Marriage functioned as an important social and economic contract in both societies. And both held up marriage to be one of the most sacred institutions in their historical context. Thus, it is not surprising why sociologists and anthropologists study marriage to understand societies.

But marriage is not only valuable for ancient society or for medieval society. Marriage is a key social indicator for the present age as well. If one wants to study social values and the social character of a society, one needs to study the nature of marriage and its function in that society. For instance, when one sees how people marry in the United States, one can understand the values of that society. Who marries whom? When do they get married? What is the nature of the wedding ceremony? Who is generally invited? Who is not invited? Who administers the wedding, generally? Who are the two parties to marriage? What kind of a marriages is allowed? A marriage between which individuals is generally frowned upon? What is the nature of marriage laws? Which marriage laws are being changed and how? A society's understanding of marriage and desire for a particular direction in marriage laws indicate the ethos of the people. Thus, in the United States, it is significant that nearly every state that introduces the anti-homosexual marriage clause in their state constitution has it approved by the general electorate on a state-wide vote. This means that the majority of the Americans not only believe that marriage between the same sex is wrong, but that they believe that it should be criminalized. This is a picture into the American perception of homosexuality as a practice. Outlawing homosexual marriage bond in a state-wide vote indicates that the voters are desirous of outlawing homosexuality itself. Because marriage practices and the perception of marriage laws are indicators of the societal value at any given time and in any given place, the new direction of American voters to criminalize homosexuality in marriage shows a targeted direction of the American people. Outlawing of homosexual marriage has been a factor for Democrat states as well as Republican states, so it seems like it is a non-partisan issue, at least as the people (or the voters) are concerned. The fact that American people are actively outlawing the homosexual marriage bond by plebiscite vote at this time in history indicates what direction they want their country to go. Marriage practices and perceptions of marriage laws are key indicators of societal values.

The reason why marriage is such a key indicator of a society is that there is a permanency about marriage. Of course, there are a lot of divorces in America. But one will be hard-pressed to find those who are getting married counting on getting a divorce. The understanding is that they want to get married for life. They are getting married because they want to spend the rest of their life with the person they are marrying. People do not go into marriage, expecting the marriage to break up. Thus, there is a permanency about marriage. Permanency is the ideal. The parties going into marriage expect permanency. In the midst of all the uncertainties that characterize human life, marriage is seen as the most final or permanent of all things human.

Even in terms of social practices, marriage seems to be the most permanent. A person generally tends to stay married to the same person more than they are "married" to their jobs. People may change their job quite often in America, but not many change their marriage partners so frequently. Not only do people change their jobs more frequently than their marriage, people change their homes more than their marriage. Thus, it is possible to find people who have moved a few times in their life time although it is not so easy to find people in large numbers who have married different people as much. Whether Americans are consciously thinking about it or not, their actions and life confirm the relative permanency of the marriage bond vis-à-vis all other social practices. This is the case outside of America as well. This is certainly true in Europe and Asia. And this is also the case in other continents.

In the same way that marriage is crucial for understanding a society in any given time and at any given place, marriage is crucial for understanding the Korean-American identity. What is the key value related to marriage for Korean-Americans? Generally, all will agree that the expectation of marrying a person with a Korean origin is the highest value in the Korean society for marriage. In a sense, it is a given in many cases. Koreans are expected to marry Koreans. Historically, Korean parents have even disowned their children for marrying white. Even today, when Korean parents talk about marriage, they tell their children that they should marry a Korean. Marrying a Korean is an expectation not only of the parents but also of other adults in the Korean-American community. Many Korean-American adults will shake their head and gossip behind the scene when they see a couple who is mixed, racially. But it is not the older generation that balks at intermarriages. Even the younger generation of Korean-Americans prefer not to see intermarriages. With the younger generation, there is a complication (at least in comparison to the perception of the parents). The younger generation may view themselves as more "Asian" and "Asian-American" than Korean-American, so for them intermarriage is marrying someone who is not Asian. Thus, in this paradigm, marrying a white person is intermarriage, but marrying a Chinese-American would not be seen as intermarriage. Often, Korean-American parents are not aware of the new dynamics in identity among Korean-American youth. Most Korean-American parents assume that their children will marry a Korean so they almost rarely broach the topic.

Although Korean-Americans may not introduce the topic of marriage in conversations with their children, they seriously want their children to marry Korean. This is one of the central reasons why Korean-American parents force their children to attend a Korean-American church and actively participate in a Korean-

American youth group. Korean-American parents bring their children to a Korean-American church so that they could meet other Korean-Americans. They want their children to make Korean-American friends. They want their children to stay in the Korean-American community via the Korean-American church and friendships formed within that context. They hope that as their children interact with Korean-Americans in a distinctively Korean context that they will eventually marry Koreans. They expect the Korean-American church to be the social catalyst for their children's marriage to a person of Korean descent.

Now that we have identified the object of their desire, let us consider some of the mechanics involved in the creation of Korean-American marriages. Traditionally, Koreans have often opted for arranged marriages. Even in post-Korean War modern Korea, many Koreans have favored a type of arranged marriage to a marriage resulting from a type of the American dating system. But it is important to note that modern arranged marriages are different from its predecessor, the traditional Korean arranged marriage system. In the traditional arranged marriage system, the persons marrying did not have much say. Thus, if the parents wanted their daughter to marry a guy from the town over, they would talk with the parents and the arrangements would be finalized by the parents. Often, the marriage arrangements were conducted without the input of the children. Even when children's opinions were consulted, it was the parents who had the final say and the children were expected to obey the decision of the parents. Feelings or "love" did not figure into the marriage arrangement. It was a type of a social contract.

In modern Korea, however, the traditional type of arranged marriage system was abandoned in lieu of a revised arranged marriage system. In the new arranged marriage system, which in Korean is called "Joong-May," the parents of the man (or the woman) wanting to get married approach the parents of the potential marriage partner. They provide details of their child and receive details of the child of the parents whom they have approached. If they both agree to go forward with "Joong-May," then they would arrange for their children to meet in a "blind date" somewhere. Often, the blind date is arranged at a restaurant. The son and his potential marriage partner meet at the restaurant and talk over dinner. Since the parents have both approved the marriage, it is up to the two potential partners to decide whether to go ahead with the "arranged marriage." If both the son and the daughter decide after the arranged blind date to get married, then the engagement ceremony date will be set. The two will become boyfriend and girlfriend after their "yes" is registered and transmitted to the other party. They will be boyfriend and girlfriend until the date of the engagement ceremony. In the Korean tradition, the engagement ceremony is a very important affair. Parents of the engaging individuals invite all their friends and family member. It is often as big as the wedding itself. When the engagement ceremony is concluded along with the engagement feast, the two individuals become officially "fiancée." After the engagement ceremony, a wedding date is set. In the Korean tradition, it is a social taboo to break off the engagement. When a person goes through the engagement ceremony, the person is no longer available and is seen as basically married to his fiancée. Only an incident of epic proportions could justify breaking off of the engagement. In this, the Korean society (as well as all other Asian societies) is completely different from the American society and European countries. Engagement is not seen as serious in the West, whereas engagement is like marriage in Asia. One of the reasons for this may be due to the fact that marriage has been a sacrament for such a long time in Europe. Marriage itself is the sacred moment. Everything up to that moment is not seen as sacred. Thus, in western wedding ceremonies, there is often an opportunity for the attendees to object to the Holy Matrimony. If no one objects at that given moment, the clergyman will say, "May everyone forever hold their peace" – meaning, "if you did not speak up this moment to object to the wedding, once the Holy Matrimony is finalized, you have no right to object to the marriage." Often, clergyman concludes the wedding by saying, "What God has joined together, let not men separate." There is finality to marriage after the wedding ceremony is concluded. This conception is missing in Asia because Asia has not had a Christian history. Marriage is not a sacrament for the majority of Koreans and other Asians. Although the marriage ceremony is special and even can be called "sacred," the marriage ceremony is not more special or more sacred than the engagement ceremony. For most Koreans, the engagement ceremony is, in fact, more sacred than marriage because it is the moment when the intent for Holy Matrimony has been finalized. There is no turning back, unless there is an earth-shaking epic tragedy or transgression. In this, the Korean culture can be seen as similar to the traditional Jewish religion. In ancient Jewish societies, when a person was betrothed to be married (engaged), that person was seen to be basically married. In fact, many experts of Jewish Law equate the engagement ceremony with the wedding ceremony in Rabbinc Judaism. Someone who is engaged is expected to follow through the wedding ceremony. There is no talk of abandoning the fiancée at the altar. It is unthinkable. Similar to traditional Judaism, the Korean community views engagement ceremony as on par with the marriage ceremony. Thus, if a man or a woman does not want to get married, they better stop the process before the engagement ceremony where all friends and family members will be invited. Breaking off the wedding after the engagement ceremony is concluded is taboo in the Korean society. Even if there are epic transgressions and they may have legitimate reasons for breaking off the engagement, those who initiate the break off of the engagement are often seen as the bad guys in the deal and they will often be shunned. Their good name will be tarnished and they will suffer social consequences in the Korean society, in most cases.

  The idea is that because the parents have agreed to the wedding and the two parties in the marriage have agreed to the wedding, they should follow through on the bond they have agreed to. In a way, one can see the influence of Confucianism in Korean marriage practices. Many assume the whole process to be a part of heaven's ordained course of events. Once the parties to marriage agree to marriage in oral agreement, this oral contract is deemed to be sacred and binding. Unlike the American society, in Confucian Asian society, oral agreement is far more sacred than written agreements. In fact, written agreements are seen as an insult to Confucian sensibilities and impede good human relations. Many western businessmen have learned with bitter tears this reality. Often, westerners who push to have Japanese CEO's sign on the dotted line lose the contracts that they have won. When Japanese bosses agree to make a business deal verbally, that should be seen as set in stone. Details and the written contract are not seen as important. Efforts to push a written contract to support the oral contract will only offend Japanese and Chinese sensibilities. There has to be tact that written contracts are not privileged because Confucian individuals see this as an insult to their personhood. Thus, it would not be surprising for a Chinese company or a Japanese company to abandon an orally agreed contract if the western partner aggressively pushes for a written contract and insult their Confucian ways. The insult is what breaks the Oral Contract because the insult is great in the Confucian system. Basically, Confucian individuals will believe that westerners have no respect for them as individuals and do not trust them. Since Confucianism is a system based on human relationships, this insult is the greatest insult. Many Chinese and Japanese corporations will care less if their western business partner is morally corrupt in terms of sexual practices or even indicted by their government on various charges. Since Confucianism emphasizes human relationships, Chinese and Japanese companies will not abandon their obligations in human relationships over something they perceive to be small like criminal charges or other "moral" problems. But when western companies aggressively push for a written contract to confirm the oral contract, this is a serious insult that cannot be forgiven by many Confucian individuals. Thus, Confucian companies will go with a more disadvantageous business deal with someone who will respect the Confucian ways. This was clearly the case in the history of the relationship between Japanese businesses and American businesses. Many companies in America lost profitable contracts because of their transgression against Confucian ways. And this will be the case for many Chinese companies now that China is emerging as the Japan of this century.

The important Confucian principle of honoring the oral agreement applies to the marriage as well. If the two families give tacit approval to the marriage and the two parties involved agree with a firm "yes," then the marriage has to happen. Any disruption, barring a catastrophic event, is unthinkable. Many Koreans marry in this new-type of arranged marriage system ("Joong-May"). What is different in the new arranged marriage system from the traditional Korean arranged marriage system is that under the new system, the man and the woman who are actually getting married have a say in their marriage. Even if the parents have agreed to introduce their children for potential marriage, if one of the potential marriage partners say "no," then the marriage will not happen. Thus, the first blind date is crucial. Generally, within 24 hours after the first blind date, the intent for marriage will be expressed. The son will tell his parents that he wants to marry her. And the daughter will tell her parents that she agrees to marry him. Once the "yes" is registered with the parents, they will share the news with each other. Then, the oral agreement is made. The engagement ceremony date will be quickly set.

There are cases where the parties of "Joong-May" hold off giving a firm "yes," but this is frowned upon. Both parties are interested in knowing whether it is a "yes" or whether it is a "no." They are not interested in a "maybe." Thus, in most "Joong-May," both of the parties will know within 24 hours if the arranged marriage (agreed on previously by the parents) will go forward with the confirmation of their children. In very rare cases, the man or the woman may request to see each other a few more times to see if they are sure. But since "Joong-May" is not meant to be a date system, seeing each other 3 more times without a firm "yes" is generally the maximum. If there is no firm "yes" after 3 times of meeting, then the "Joong-May" will break off. Both of the parties may get offended and certainly the side that is receiving the hesitation will feel personal insult after 3 meetings. Thus, "Joong-May" must be seen as existing completely for the purpose of marriage. It is not meant to help two people fall in love. The assumption is that love will grow with each passing day once they make the firm commitment. Such is the order of Heaven under the Confucian system. Even if they are not consciously thinking that they are acting in Confucian ways, they have internalized Confucianism in their psyche since Confucianism has been the dominant philosophy in East Asia for over a millennium.

Of course, not all Korean-American youths subscribe to the system of "Joong-May." Many refuse to have their parents initiate the process in the first place. However, surprisingly, even many Korean-Americans youth eventually marry through "Joong-May." This is the case with even American-born Korean-Americans. Of course, they may not know how the system operates in all of its details, but those Korean-Americans who submit to the system know enough to operate within the general structure of the "Joong-May" system. Their parents explain what they must do before they go on the blind date. And after the blind date, their parents ask their child whether the answer is "yes" or "no." Since the parents are more tied to Korean ways, they will use their children's input of "yes" or "no" and transmit the information to the parents of the potential partner and they will negotiate using Korean ways. They will direct their children according to the "Joong-May" system. Often, Korean-American children do not know that their parents are cleverer than they appear to them. The Korean-American parents are playing with many pieces on the chessboard with the fundamental rules being that of the "Joong-May" system. Their children are often oblivious participants in the process. But many happy marriages occur through a revised Joong-May system to accommodate the complexities of the Korean experience in America, including the fact that many Korean-Americans are born in the United States and cannot even speak Korean. Many Korean-

Americans of the MTV generation surprisingly submit to the Joong-May system. In a typical Korean-American church, at least 30 per cent of the American-born Korean-Americans have married through the Joong-May system revised to fit the complexities of the Korean-American experience.

Although Joong-May is often arranged by the parents themselves, there are marriage brokers who actually bring the parents together. There are societal marriage brokers now, although this was less common in the past. Because of the population explosion and the greater mobility of the Korean masses, marriage brokers have emerged to bring families of like backgrounds together according to a type of Confucian system. The two families will meet first and then approve the arrangement. They will thereafter arrange for the blind date between their children. And then the process of Joong-May will go forward as if the two parents met on their own and arranged the marriage themselves. The rules will be the same as if they conducted Joong-May on their own without the marriage broker.

Although the concept of the marriage broker for pay is a fairly recent phenomenon in Korea, there have always been marriage brokers in post-Korean War modern Korea. Most often, these marriage brokers were heads of villages or small towns, in the case that the parties are not Christians. In the case of Christians, marriage brokers tended almost exclusively to be senior pastors of churches. Thus, a family which wants their son to get married would approach the senior pastor and ask for "Joong-May." The senior pastor would look for a suitable wife based on the family's background and the son's achievements. He will first introduce the best possible candidate. If both parties agree to go through with the Joong-May process, then a blind date will be set up. If both parties agree to the arranged marriage after the blind date, then an engagement ceremony date will be set and the marriage will go forward. If one of the parties does not agree, then the senior pastor will introduce the second choice candidate to the parents who initiated the marriage brokerage. His obligations are to the parents who brought the request.

Obviously, the first choice woman whom he introduced who said "no" may want the senior pastor to be the official broker and her parents may approach the senior pastor with this purpose as well. But it is possible that she already has a marriage broker. Maybe she attends another church and her parents have approached their senior pastor for marriage brokerage. When the two senior pastors who are marriage brokers for their own congregations (say in New York and Los Angeles) meet at the denominational meeting in Chicago, they can compare notes and see whom they can broker in marriage. It may seem like a complex system, but it really is not since senior pastors, ever since the beginning of the Korean church some 100 years ago, played the role of the marriage broker. Senior pastors are expected to play the role of marriage brokers. In fact, for many church members, that is one of his most important functions.

While many Koreans and even many Korean-Americans marry through the new arranged marriage system of "Joong-May," there is a sizable number of Korean-Americans who marry through the more Americanized dating system. It is possible to see why this could be the case for some Korean-Americans since they grew up in the United States and many Korean-Americans were born on American soil. They grew up seeing Hollywood movies and TV. And the mass media seemed to highlight the dating process as the normative process. Since many Korean-American parents do not talk to their children about dating or marriage, many Korean-American teenagers do not have any other way to learn about dating and marriage, except from mass media. Perhaps, it is important to examine the role of Korean-American parents in the framing of Korean-American youth value system in terms of dating, as it will shed light on the perception of Korean-American youth and their identity.

Korean-American parents do not normally talk about dating or marriage. There are several reasons for this. First of all, Korean culture does not welcome conversations about dating or marriage. In the Korean culture, marriage is presumed to be sacred. It is expected that Koreans will marry Koreans. It is expected that Koreans will find a suitable spouse to meet the expectations of the parents. It is expected that the children not marry anyone whom the parents object to. These are basically all givens of the Korean society. Since this is presumed to be true and everyone understands the unspoken rules regarding marriage, there is no real need to expound on the unspoken rule. At least, that is what many Korean parents think. Thus, for much of junior and high school life, there will not be talk of marriage. Only when children are of marriageable age will Korean parents talk about marriage. But even then, they will not talk about the rules of the marriage that is set in stone at least in terms of the Oral Law. They will talk in terms of the need for their children to get married soon. Thus, it is the urgency of marriage that will prompt the talk. Even as Korean parents tell their children to get married as soon as possible, they will assume that their children will not marry anyone whom they will object to for marriage. It is because the Oral Law about marriage is assumed and understood ubiquitously by Koreans all over the world that Korean parents assume that there need not be an exposition about it. And since the Korean society is an amalgamation of Korean families who feel this way, Korean society, by in large, militates against talk of dating and marriage. Many Korean families will consider a detailed conversation regarding marriage a taboo topic.

There are other reasons why Korean parents do not talk about dating or marriage. Many Korean parents do not want their children to date before college so they do not talk about it. Some parents will tell their children not to have any girlfriends in high school. But most will assume that their children know this. And they will not even bring it up because they may feel that talking about it will only raise their interest about having a girlfriend and will lead to the temptation of dating. Korean parents want their high school students to be focused on studies. Since academic achievement – or success in formal education – is one of the most important Confucian values, typical Korean parents will expect their children to focus all their attention on this goal. Most Korean parents view having a girlfriend or even a special female friend as antithetical to the potential for academic success. For them, it is impossible to spend much time with a girlfriend and be academically number one at school.

There is another reason why Korean parents do not talk about dating or marriage with their children. In the case of Korean-Americans, many parents of Korean-American youth are too busy trying to make a living as immigrants in America to spend time to talk about dating and marriage over a long period of time. Dating and marriage is not the kind of topic that you introduce and drop; it requires conversations over a period of time. Children can have many questions about dating and marriage. There can be related questions regarding sex and other teenage issues related to dating. The conversation can become very complicated with topics focusing on potential dating partners and marriage partners. Many Korean-American parents do not feel that they have the time or the mental energy to engage their children in conversations about such complex subjects.

For many who are not a part of the Korean-American community, it may be difficult to understand the predicament of Korean-American parents. Many Korean-American parents are immigrants and they are establishing themselves in the New Land. This means that many of them came to America with nothing and with only the shirt on their backs, so to speak. From nothing, they had not only to make a living to survive but also to make enough to provide good education for their kids. Good education for Korean-Americans means being in good neighborhoods with good high schools. For many Korean-Americans, this means affluent white suburbia, where houses are the most expensive in the region. Korean-American parents thus work a typical 14 hour shift per day to arrive at a level of income that will allow them to live in good white neighborhoods with good educational systems.

A typical Korean family starts out living in a very dangerous neighborhood when they first arrive in the USA. They do not have much money to start with, and they lack any credit history in the USA that would allow them to borrow money from American banks. It is easier to get housing without a credit history and a large sum of deposit money in dangerous neighborhoods. Also, it is easier to start businesses in dangerous neighborhoods because no one wants to work there. Most Korean-American shop owners working in very dangerous neighborhoods have had gun pointed at them more than twice in the last 5 years. Many Korean-American store owners get shot and some even die. This is not uncommon. But because nobody wants to start businesses in such dangerous areas, Korean-Americans find it financially viable to start a business in these dangerous neighborhoods. For instance, the rent for store space is cheaper. And since transportation out of bad neighborhoods is not very good, Korean-American store owners in rough neighborhoods have ready customers for their goods. Wal Mart and other big stores generally do not enter very dangerous neighborhoods. Thus, while Wal Mart and other big stores cut into the profit of small stores in the area, they cannot touch very dangerous neighborhoods. Thus, dangerous neighborhoods provide recent Korean-American immigrants with a chance at business success. The profit margin may be small but the competition from Wal Mart and other big stores are minimal or non- existent.

When Korean-Americans make enough money working 14 hour shifts per day 6-7 days per week, the first thing they do is to move into an affluent white neighborhood for the education of their kids. Korean-American parents will drive 1 hour with joy to ensure that their children are not going to all black high schools or all Hispanic high schools. These Korean-Americans understand that all black high schools and all Hispanic high schools do not get much money from the state for their high schools so their high school programs are far inferior to a typical high school in an all white neighborhood. Korean-American parents are looking out for the educational interests of their children. They are not interested in making social reforms in a given area because they are immigrants, but they want their children to get the best education possible. For Korean-Americans, the solution is moving to an all white neighborhood with a good educational system already in place. In order to make mortgage payments on time, Korean-American parents work very hard. Since they live in affluent white suburbs, they need to drive 1 hour or more to depressed black neighborhoods where they had started their business. Thus, they are adding more hours to their 14 hour work day. And since they are now in white neighbhordhoods, they feel an obligation to purchase expensive cars. Whereas owning luxury cars was not a social necessity when they lived in a poor neighborhood, it became a social necessity to keep up (at least visibly) with affluent white neighbhors. Thus, typically, Korean-American families never take a vacation. Korean-American parents are always working to ensure that their children get the best education possible in the USA. They are trying to be the best parents possible by the rules of Confucianism that has become a part of their psyche.

Because of the duty-driven rigorous work schedule, many Korean-American parents are too tired to carry on serious conversations with their children when they come home. For instance, Korean-American parents who operate a dry cleaning business leave home at 6 AM and arrive back home at 8 PM. This means that they will most likely not see their children off to school, and they will not be home when their children come home from school. In fact, they will have dinner at 8 PM when they get back from work. Their children would have had dinner before that in most cases. Korean-American parents are too tired to talk to their children about serious topics. In most cases, Korean-American parents will ask their children if they studied and did their homework. And many Korean-American parents will expect their children to eat in relative silence. Many Korean-American parents are too tired to tolerate constant chatter from their children. This may seem harsh to white American parents who work 8 hours per day in a nicely airconditioned room with a comfortable chair and secretaries to make coffee and take dictations, but it is understandable to many Korean-Americans who share this similar work experience and know what it means to stand for most of the 14 hours of a typical workday as they work with only a thirty minute lunch break and other food breaks throughout the torturous work day. Obviously, there are some Korean-Americans who do make a concerted effort to talk to their children after they come back from work. They can talk about the day and carry on other small chatter. But a serious topic of conversation, such as about dating and marriage, may feel too stressful to initiate and maintain.

Related to the demands of the immigrant life is the problem of communication. Because Korean-American families represent Korean immigrants to the United States and their children, it is only natural that the parents of Korean-American youth who immigrated to the USA as adults will have problems communicating in the English language. Their children born in the USA will not have a problem with English language communication, but many of them will not know enough Korean to communicate with their parents about things beyond simple, mundane things in life. Dating and marriage involve topics that will stretch vocabulary usage (either in the English language or in the Korean language), so effective communication breaks down. In many cases, Korean-American parents do not have the needed English vocabulary, particularly colloquial English vocabulary, to maintain effective communication with their English speaking children. And many Korean-American youth are deficient in their ability to communicate in Korean so they cannot express their thoughts and questions effectively, and furthermore, they will not be able to understand what their parents are saying in Korean, fully.

But the unwillingness of the Korean-American parents to talk about dating and marriage (or their inability to do so because of work fatigue or language problems) is not the only impediments to discussions about dating and marriage. Korean-American youth often do not want to talk about dating and marriage with their parents. There are several reasons why Korean-American youth do not want to talk about dating and marriage with their parents. First of all, it is important that Korean-American youth are educated in the United States by American educational system, American cultural values, and the mass media. What this means is that Korean-American youth will share some of the hang-ups of non-Korean-American youth born and raised in the United States. One characteristic nature of the American teenager angst is the refusal to communicate with parents about deep, personal issues. For better or for worse, many Korean-American teenagers share a reluctance to share their thoughts and questions with their parents relating to dating and marriage. They may ask their friends or talk to their diary about it, but they would be hesitant to approach their parents. This is typical of many teenagers in the USA. Often, many white American parents develop a way of communicating with their children that involves a type of psychologist's ability to pry open their children's deepest thoughts, feelings, and sentiments. Since most teenagers in the USA will not volunteer their personal thoughts, many American parents are left to guess what their children think or to try to find a way to encourage them to open themselves up. Parents of Korean-American teenagers face similar obstacles as parents of white Americans in this regard. Korean-American teens are in many ways "normal teens" of America. They were born in the USA and think like a typical American teenager. The difference is that they are not white and they will never be fully accepted as white. They are visibly Asian and that will always play a role throughout their lives in the American context. It is impossible for Korean-Americans to rid themselves of their visible Koreanness.

    Besides typical American teenage angst which prevents open dialogue between America's teenagers from communicating with their parents, Korean-American teenagers feel a type of cultural gap with their parents who came to the United States after they reached their adulthood. Many Korean-American teenagers feel that they cannot identity with their parents. There is the primary factor of the language gap. Parents of Korean-American youth cannot speak English very well. Having grown up in America, Korean-American youth expect people in America to speak English. Many Korean-American teenagers will not have problem saying that those who do not speak English well and have no interest in learning it should "go back to where they came from." Since many Korean-American youth are educated in affluent white neighborhoods, they share the societal mores of these neighorhoods. Whereas if they grew up in Hispanic neighborhoods, they may not say this so readily, if they grew up in *gringo* neighborhoods, it would only seem natural to them based on their suburbia education that anyone wanting to live in America should learn to speak English. Of course, most Korean-Americans who think or say that those Mexicans who do not want to learn English should "go back to where they came from" will not say this to Koreans, even if they encounter FOB's ("Fresh Off the Boat"). In a sense, many Korean-American teens live a dual existence. They grew up in white neighborhoods and were educated in white neighborhoods, so their societal value system is largely similar to those of white American teens. But there is this whole world of the Korean-American immigrants to which they belong to whether they want to or not. So, even if they meet in a youth group comprised 100% of Korean-Americans educated in white neighborhoods and they all collectively share a white view of the value of the English language, they cannot escape the fact that the parents of most of the youth group members will not speak even basic English for communication. For many Korean-American teens, this duality is tacitly ignored. But that does not mean that this duality eludes them completely. At least in the subconscious, if not poignantly in the conscious, Korean-American teens view their parents with disdain. Although they may be too afraid to utter even to themselves that their parents should "go back to where they came from" for refusing to learn English, many Korean-American teens have a sentiment in this direction. In other words, many Korean-American teens have a disdain for the Koreanness of their parents. Of course, most Korean-American parents are completely unaware of this. This is understandable since most Korean-American parents do not have a clue what white American discourse is on the general level and in America's suburban high schools. Just because Korean-American parents are not aware of the thought process of their children does not mean that they are not an integral part of the cognitive process and the epistemological outlook of their children. The conscious or submerged disdain for their parents who came to America as adults often prevent Korean-American teens from approaching them for advice or opinions on all kinds of issues, including dating and marriage.

Besides the latent (or overt) disdain that many Korean-American youth feel toward their parents who immigrated from Korea in the realm of language, Korean-American youth often see their parents' conservative value system as backward or outdated. Unlike white American teenagers who may feel this way about their parents, Korean-Americans configure their parents' "backwardness" in terms of Korean ways. It is important to understand that many Korean-American youths are introduced to surface American culture, which actually may appear very liberal. But underneath the surface is the conservative Puritan way of the American people. American culture is considered very conservative by comparative sociologists and cultural anthropologists. But many Korean-Americans are not exposed to the deeper level of the American society; they only know what they see in TV and movies. Even if they have good white friends, many Korean-Americans never really enter the inner sanctum of white American culture that has deep roots in Puritanism and Catholicism – both trends share similarity in conservative attitudes towards sex, marriage, and all kinds of other societal values. In other words, many Korean-American teens get fed the secular agenda in their public high schools and do not really get to know the real American culture that forms the foundation of the American society. Whereas white Americans often experience refracting of these secular values (from public schools) in the context of their family life, Korean-Americans assume these secular values to be the norms in the

American society. Obviously, MTV is not typical of Americans and Hollywood movies do not describe a typical value system in the American context. Americans may see MTV as an outlet and go to the movies to indulge their fantasies, but in real life many Americans behave in a very conservative way. Puritan and Catholic heritages cannot be written off in America. But many Korean-Americans do not know this. It is outside of their experience. They learn things from MTV, Hollywood movies, and in their secular education and then they go home to a Korean household. So, they assume that their Korean immigrant household is abnormal. They are missing the experience of the inner sanctum of conservative white American family life, where Puritan-based and Catholic-influenced family values are inculcated. Since Korean-American youth do not experience the inner life of a typical white American family, they cannot know how it is. Based on this ignorance, many Korean-American teens assume that their Korean immigrant parents are backward and all of their value system useless and "Third World."

The upshot is that Korean-American teens do not have the opportunity to discuss dating and marriage with their parents. A myriad of factors – ranging from the rigorous immigrant work schedule to Korean-American teenage misunderstanding of real American mores – preclude effective dialogue between Korean-American teens and their parents. Thus, Korean-American teens are heavily influenced by Hollywood and the mass media in terms of their worldviews on dating and marriage. It is, therefore, no surprise that many Korean-American teens resort to a dating system described in American movies and TV. They think that that is the normal way things are done in America.

Interestingly enough, many Korean-Americans start dating non-Koreans. One of the reasons for this is that there are not many Koreans in their high schools. Thus, Korean-Americans will date whites. It is possible that they may date individuals of other ethnic backgrounds, such as Hispanics or other Asians. Rarely will Korean-Americans date African-Americans. Besides the fact that many Korean-Americans do not go to high schools with many African-Americans, there is hostility against African-Americans because many Korean-American merchants suffer seriously in African-American neighborhoods and some even get shot to death working in these dangerous, economically depressed neighborhoods.

Often, the Korean-American experimentation with dating in high school ends in tears. Besides the travails of teenage life that impede the teenager dating scene, many Korean-Americans experience their first painful self-awareness of the significance of their color in their dating life. By nature, dating life can be quite intimate. It is easier for all kinds of guards to be down in the context of an intimate relationship. Things can be said off guard. Many times, Korean-American teens come to hear comments against their color and ethnicity in the context of dating. They find out that their visible difference as Korean-Americans has a bearing on their identity and perception by others. Previously, they did not think that their visible Koreanness mattered. They have been lulled by the secular lie that "color doesn't matter." The dating relationship (particularly with a white individual) tears them away from their Santa-Clausian belief about color in the United States. Of course, it is important to note that their white girlfriend is not necessarily being intentionally racist. It is possible that in the heated fight between lovers comments will fly. Maybe the Korean guy said that his white girlfriend chews like a horse. Being angry, the white girlfriend might say that the Korean guy has eyes more slanted (or "Chinkier") than the leaning tower of Pisa. She may not have meant anything by it. Maybe the white girlfriend insulted him with the first thing she noticed. But that is precisely the point. She *noticed* the fact that her Korean boyfriend had slanted eyes. Whereas she would never have said that to him if he were not her boyfriend, she teased that feature of his because she was "pissed off" at her boyfriend who made a comment about the way she chews. Even after having said it, she as a white person may think that it was a fair insult after the insult that she received. Of course, for the Korean boyfriend, it would really hurt. He can think to himself that the white girlfriend can change the way she chews but he cannot change his Asian-looking slanted eyes. It is at this moment that he would realize the fact of his Koreanness, poignantly. In the like manner, many Korean-American teens experience the harsh fact of their visible Koreanness in the context of dating non-Koreans in high school.

When Korean-American teens encounter self-awareness of their color and Koreanness via their significant other, they either start moving toward greater denial or in the other direction of solidarity with other Korean-Americans. Interestingly enough, when some Korean-American teens are insulted about their visible Koreanness, they start trying to be "more white" to compensate for their Koreanness. They can even become hostile to Korean ways and other Koreans, such as the FOB's ("Fresh Off the Boat" Koreans). Some, therefore, indulge themselves in self-hatred. They work harder and harder for acceptance by the white world. In the process they turn their back on all things Korean, including even their parents (in extreme cases).

While some Korean-American teens go toward the direction of self-hatred and compensation, other Korean-Americans take the "screw this" attitude toward the white world. These Korean-American teens believe that they should cut their losses while they are ahead. Thus, they abandon the white world as their primary matrix of identity and socializing. They start gravitating toward other Koreans. In the case that there are not enough Korean-Americans in their high school, they start befriending other Asian-Americans (such as Chinese-Americans and Korean-Americans). They may even start going to a Korean school on Saturdays in an effort to reconnect with their Korean roots. They may become more and more actively involved with their Korean-American church – more for ethnic participation than for Christian growth. They may request that their parents expose them to Korean experiences, such as a trip to South Korea to visit their Korean relatives.

What this means is that there are two resultant trends in the dating process. There will be a group of Korean-Americans who will look forward to dating only non-Koreans. Many of them will be pursuing non-Korean partners because they are trying to compensate for their Koreanness which is under attack. In the Korean-American community, these individuals are seen as "Bananas" – those who are yellow on the outside and white on the inside. Of course, there is a simple measure to see if a Korean-American is dating a white woman because he hates himself and all things Korean or for some other reason besides self-hatred. If Korean-Americans dating whites bring their white girlfriends to Korean contexts, then it is possible to say that he is not indulging in his self-hatred of Koreanness. This does not, of course, change the fact that Koreans present may not appreciate his bringing a white woman to Korean contexts, especially as "a girlfriend to flaunt."

The other direction in dating is dating of Korean-Americans or others who are visibly Asian. This trend is greater among Asian-Americans in general and Korean-Americans in particular. Bad dating experiences with whites often drive Korean-Americans toward their ethnic group. Thus, by the time that Korean-Americans reach college, they prefer dating Korean-Americans or other Asian-Americans. For those who pursue active dating with view to marriage will naturally end up marrying a Korean-American or an Asian-American.

There are some Korean-Americans who find their spouse through dating, and these two trends are the most dominant among Korean-Americans who prefer to choose their spouse through dating. But it must be stressed that surprisingly many Korean-Americans do not marry via the dating process. In fact, many Korean-Americans, even those who are born and bred in America and who cannot speak a word of Korean, opt to utilize a form of the Joong-May system. This does not mean, of course, that they did not date at all. In fact, many Korean-Americans date post-college. But many find that the dating system is an inadequate way to find a life partner.

It is interesting to examine why many Korean-Americans find the dating system inadequate for finding a wife or a husband. By the time that many Korean-Americans reach the age of marriage, they have reached maturity. Many reached this stage through much social and cultural rejection. The pain has taken a toll on their person and psyche. They want things to be simpler and not complex. They reflect on the complexities of the dating system. So, many Koreans opt to go toward marriage with a clear goal of marriage in mind. They have done the "romance thing" and they realized that it was temporary or temporarily gratifying. They want something more permanent, so they look toward marriage. They realize that marriage via dating will take a long time. They have been there, so they know. The Joong-May system is relatively simple. You meet someone who may be compatible to you. There are no hidden surprises. You are told their family background, their level of education, their interests and hobbies, etc. before meeting. The person has been approved by your parents, which may play an increasing role of significance with each maturing year. So, you go into a Joong-May system, ready to get married. When you see someone you like, you simply make a commitment to marry that person within a few dates at most. This seems remarkably simple compared to the complexities and the heartaches of dating life. Some even see innocence and purity to the Joong-May system. Because the commitment for marriage is made relatively soon, there is no real time for heartaches and resentments to enter – for instance, due to the perceived lack of interest in making a real commitment to the permanency of relationship in a timely manner. The parties being introduced for marriage probably do not have much time outside of their professional goal to "make it" in America, so they probably do not get many opportunities to come across dating partners, any way. Thus, the Joong-May system is convenient, as well. And it is the Joong-May system most Korean-Americans opt for today when it is time for marriage.

Many Korean-Americans view the fact that even the most Banana-seeming Korean-Americans opting for the Joong-May system by the time they get married as a good thing. It helps to preserve the Korean-American community. The parents of two Korean-Americans getting married through the Joong-May system are happy because they can speak in Korean with their child's in-laws. They can attend the Korean-American church, together. They can involve themselves in predominantly Korean-American social activities. Many Korean-Americans are thrilled that their child did not marry a non-Korean and dilute the 5000 year pure Korean bloodline. They think that if their USA-born Korean-American child married a white woman they would be damned to earthly Hell of trying to understand and manage through the white world and all its complexities at most intimate moments, like "family" Thanksgiving dinner and Christmas celebrations and other types of family gatherings. They would not only have to learn better English, they will have to learn white American ways. They will have to try to get along with white parents of their daughter-in-law. Most parents of Korean-American youth are incapable of doing this because their acculturation in the American context has had the Korean-American community as their primary matrix. It is one thing to go to an impersonal formal dinner once a while and hobnob with a bunch of white people, who require superficial acquaintance. It is something completely different to get to know the white in-laws and experience the typical kind of family conflicts that exist in all families and in-law relationship. Whereas if the in-laws were Korean, things can be smoothed over easily, the fact that the in-laws are white creates conflicts on all kinds of levels – color, ethnic background, culture, language, etc. – that cannot easily be resolved. In fact, various factors in the complex relationship are likely to compound all the existing problems.

For most Korean-Americans, having to work with non-Korean in-laws is not much of a problem yet because most Korean-Americans still opt to marry Korean-Americans or other Asian-Americans. Most Korean-Americans still opt for the Joong-

May system for the purpose of marriage. Of course, the number of intermarriages between Korean-Americans and whites is increasing. It is possible to see a rise of intermarriages between Korean-Americans and whites in the coming years. But one thing will remain a constant; that is, Korean-American parents prefer that their children marry Korean-Americans. For Korean-Americans, as it is with most other ethnicities, marriage is a key indicator of their identity and ability to perpetuate that identity. If their child married non-Korean, their Korean-American identity will end with their grandchild. They will be lost in oblivion insofar as Koreanness is involved. This has been the case with a lot of famous Koreans who married white, including the first President of Korea, Syngman Rhee. His children and descendants are no longer associated with Korea or anything Korean. The line of Syngman Rhee is forgotten and deemed no longer to exist. It is as if the Korean line of Syngman Rhee died with his death. This is the way most Korean-Americans view their family line. This clearly shows that marriage provides a picture into a society's values. Likewise, dating is an indicator of society's values, especially since the reality of dating has entered the Korean-American community in a serious way.

    Dating and Marriage provide a picture of the Korean-American society and Korean-American youth search for identity. Caught between cultures – the Korean culture of their parents and the American culture that they are most comfortable with – Korean-American youth are negotiating their identity subconsciously or proactively. They are always active in this regard because they are visibly different from the dominant groups in America. They are reminded on a regular basis of that difference in school, at work, and in friendships. It is not surprising to see why many Korean-American youth dive into the safe haven of the only Korean-American social association available to them – namely, the Korean-American church. Almost all of the Korean-American youth have been to Korean-American churches at one time or another. Many Korean-American youths attend the Korean-American church on a regular basis. Some even attend the Korean-American church youth group twice per week or more. For many Korean-Americans, the Korean-American Church has been an important part of their identity formation. Interestingly enough, since Korean-American churches have historically been very pro-American, many Korean-Americans who become an active part of Korean-American churches tend to be very patriotic. It will come as no surprise to find that all the Koreans at West Point or US Naval Academy are Christians who were very active in their church. Most of them attended Korean-American churches, faithfully.

But with 9/11, the reality set in. Whereas many Korean-Americans blissfully went about their business with the assumption that America was "Christian" before 9/11, they came to question their fundamental assumptions after 9/11. Why did God allow 9/11 to happen to America? Either Christianity was false or God no longer defended America. Korean-Americans were thrown into confusion as their primary Korean-American identity marker of the Korean-American church came to be questioned as they started to question the veracity of Christianity as the Truth. 9/11 had to be explained somehow, and many Korean-Americans opted to explain 9/11 as the conclusive evidence that Christianity was a false religion. Their fundamental shaking of identity in this regard impacted their attitudes toward dating and marriage as well. As 9/11 is relatively recent, there is not much research on its impact on the Korean-Americans. This monograph is, in fact, one of the very few of its kind in the world. Hopefully, this monograph will open the way to greater research and writing on the question of post-9/11 Korean-American identity.

Conclusion

The Korean American community has been deeply impacted by 9/11 and its aftermath. For many Koreans, it brought to fore questions about communal safety in the American context because the previously held assumption as to the safety of America was broken and the concept of North Korea as an axis-of-evil power became more relevant and "real." Many began to question how this would implicate South Korean immigrants in the United States. The question regarding the safety of Koreans in America as an immigrant community came to be externalized in two completely opposing tendencies. One trend was an aggressively conservatizing trend among the church-goers, pushing even historically left-leaning Korean churches closer toward the evangelical/fundamentalist direction. The other trend went the other direction with many individual Korean Christians leaving the church and abandoning institutional Christianity altogether, thereby leaving many Korean local congregations empty. This post-9/11 trend is most noticeable among those in the late teens and in college. In this book, I have examined the sociological phenomena of the two opposite forces that have impacted Korean-American Christianity after 9/11, particularly focusing on late teen and college age Koreans.

In order to understand the current sociological phenomena, it is important to understand the larger context of the Korean-American experience. The Korean immigration history in the United States of America is over 100 years old. 1903 marks the year of first Korean immigrants to the USA. Few hundred Koreans immigrated to Hawaii as plantation workers. Although Korean immigration is over 100 years old, due to immigration restrictions on Asians by the US government, not many Koreans immigrated to the USA from 1903 to 1965. When the US government lifted the Asian immigration ban in 1965, Korean immigration to the United States began in earnest. The 1970 US Census found about 70,000 Koreans residing in the USA. About 30,000 Koreans immigrated to the USA every year, so in 1976, about 290,000 were known to be resident in the United States. The 1980 US Census numbered Koreans at 354,529.[115] In 1990, the Korean-American population was estimated to be 1.3 million.[116] Currently, there are estimated 2.1 million Koreans living in the United States. Due to majority of Korean immigrants arriving in the USA in the 1980s and 1990s, most of the Korean-Americans were either born in Korea or raised by parents born in Korea. It is not surprising, therefore, that many Korean-Americans today have primarily Korea-centric perspectives, associations, and worldviews.

Besides the Korea-centric position of the Korean-American experience, another major distinguishing characteristic of the Korean-American community is a strong Christian-centric identity. From the very beginning of Korean immigration to the USA in 1903, Korean-American communities prioritized establishment of Korean churches for their communities. For instance, from the 1903 immigration, a few hundred Korean immigrants set up a Christian church in Mokalia, Oahu in Hawaii on July 5, 1903, and another Christian church on River Street, Honolulu on November 10, 1903.[117] About 40% of the Korean immigrants were Christians but eventually most of the non-Christian Koreans became churchgoers.[118] This trend of Christian-centric identity of the Korean-American community continued throughout much of the Korean

---

[115] Won Moo Hurh and Kwang Chung Kim, *Korean Immigrants in America: A Structural Analysis of Ethnic Confinement and Adhesive Adaptation* (Rutherford: Associated University Press, 1984), p. 21.
[116] Hurh and Kim, *Korean Immigrants in America*, p. 57.
[117] Warren Y. Kim, *Koreans in America* (Seoul: Po Chin Chai Printing Co. Ltd., 1971), p. 28.
[118] Bong-Youn Choy, *Koreans in America* (Chicago: Nelson Hall, 1979), p. 77.

immigration history in the USA. In fact, Korean-American community can be seen as distinctively Christian in contradistinction to the Koreans in South Korea. *Korea Week* in Februrary, 1978, reported that only 10% of the total population in South Korea were affiliated with a Christian church. In contrast, 70% of Korean-Americans at the same time were affiliated with a Christian church in the USA.[119] It is an undeniable part of Korean-American history that Christianity has played a central role for the community, the family, and the individual. This has been true from the very beginning and holds true for the most part, even today.

One of the reasons why Korean-American churches have been effective in the Christianization of the Korean-American community is that they provide Christian worship and Korean ethnic fellowship. Hurh and Kim write: "The Korean immigrants appear, therefore, to crave both types of fellowship – spiritual (Christian) fellowship *and* ethnic fellowship.... The Korean ethnic church provides best both fellowships for the immigrant...."[120] In fact, the majority of Korean-Americans believe that these two form the primary objectives of the Korean-American church. Many, in fact, argue that the Korean-American church should not merely provide Korean ethnic fellowship but that it should also provide education for succeeding generations in Korean ways, history, and language. Yong Choon Kim writes:

> The education of the second generation of Koreans is one of the most important tasks of the Korean church for the healthy progress of the Korean-American community. For this task Korean churches in America should make a special effort to

---

[119] Hurh and Kim, *Korean Immigrants in America*, pp. 129-130.
[120] Hurh and Kim, *Korean Immigrants in America*, p. 134.

continue teaching the Korean language along with Christian education.[121]

And by in large, Korean-American churches have fulfilled their obligations in both regards. Most Korean language schools are run by Korean-American churches and not by non-Christian Korean associations or private Korean individuals. In fact, it would not be inaccurate to say that Korean-American youth born in the USA would have no exposure to things Korean apart from the family were it not for the Korean-American church. Thus, it is not surprising that Korean-American parents, even those who are not Christians themselves, encourage their children to attend a Korean-American church. The Korean-American church provides Korean-American youth not only with exposure to things Korean but also with Korean-American friends. Thus, most of the Korean-American youths would have been to a Korean-American church and were at one point or another active participants in the Korean-American church.

Because the Korean-American church is the primary center of exposure to things Korean for Korean-Americans, it is not surprising to see the heightened Koreanness resulting in anti-white sentiment. Thus, Korean-American youth have developed a term to describe Korean-American peers who prefer white friends and white settings. The term "Banana" describes Korean-American youth who are "white on the inside and yellow on the outside." Korean-American youth have themselves developed this term to ostracize fellow Korean-American youth who prefer primarily white matrix rather than a primarily Korean matrix for friendships, dating, and socio-cultural associations. Although Korean-American churches are not anti-white in any intentional way as

---

[121] Yong Choon Kim, "The Protestant Church and the Korean-American Community," *The Korean-American Community: Present and Future*, eds. Tae-Hwan Kwak and Seong Hyong Lee (Seoul: Kyungnam University Press, 1991, pp. 195-209), p. 198.

they often belong to predominantly white Christian denominations and associate frequently with white Christians and Christian organizations, the strong Korean emphasis of Korean-American churches has a natural result among the Korean-Americans toward an anti-white position.

In a sense, therefore, an anti-white position can be seen as shared by the American-born Korean-Americans and their Korean-American parents. This is most visible in the institution of the marriage. There is hardly any Korean-American parent who would not take personal offense if their children married white. In fact, most Korean-American parents specifically educate their children to marry Koreans. Most Korean-American youth prefer to associate with other Korean-Americans in terms of friendships and this trend extends to preference in marriage. Marrying a Korean is so important to Korean-Americans that a Korean-American church that encourages marriage with whites will quickly lose their legitimacy as a Korean-American church. In this sense, the Korean-American church is not much different with the African-American church.

Despite the Korean emphasis of Korean-American churches, Korean-American churches tend to be aggressively pro-American. Many Korean-American churches have not seen a distinction between being loyal to Korea as a nation and to America as a Christian nation. A part of the reason for this reality is that Korean nationalism often tended to be Christian in nature. Korean nationalism against Japanese Occupation (1910-1945) was coupled with Korean Christian resistance against Japanese imperial rule that was aggressively anti-Christian. South Korean nationalism in the Korean War was coupled with the Korean Christian resistance against North Korean and Chinese Communism which persecuted Korean Christians. Thus, when Korean-American churches uphold Korean nationalism, they uphold a type of Korean Christian nationalism. Thus, it is not in conflict of interest for Korean-Americans to be aggressively loyal to a Christian America. In fact, if push comes to shove Korean-American Christians would be more loyal to a Christian nation rather than to Korea.

In order to understand this, it is important to understand the character of Korean-American Christianity. Korean-American Christians have perpetuated a notion of a Christian America, founded by the Puritans. This has been expounded from the pulpit as well as extended within Korean-American Christian discourses in communal settings. This can be explained in part to the pervasive impact of Presbyterianism in Korea. American Presbyterian missionaries made the greatest impact on Korean Christianity. And even today, Presbyterians comprise the largest percentage of Korean Christians, followed by Korean Catholics, although Korean Catholic history is much longer than the history of Korean Presbyterianism. In fact, all the Korean Protestant denominations date the history of Christianity in Korea not from the date of the first Catholic converts but from the date of the first generation of Korean Presbyterian converts. Thus, Presbyterian-led Protestant Christianity that dominates Korean Christianity has whitewashed Korean Catholic history, including thousands of Korean Catholics martyred for their Christian faith during the Yi Dynasty by the Korean monarchy. Since the first generation of Presbyterian missionaries from Princeton Theological Seminary, Korean Presbyterianism has followed a very conservative Presbyterian route, in part because second and third generation of American missionaries tended to be conservative Presbyterians. One good example is Rev. Bruce Hunt,[122] who spent his whole life as a missionary in Korea and even was jailed by the Japanese during the Japanese Occupation along with Korean Christians. Although Rev. Bruce Hunt traces his lineage to the Princeton Presbyterian tradition, he belonged to a group of Presbyterians who broke away from Princeton Theological Seminary and founded Westminster Theological Seminary and the Orthodox Presbyterian Church. Conservative

---

[122] Rev. Bruce Hunt wrote an autobiography: Bruce F. Hunt, *For A Testimony* (Edinburgh: Banner of Truth, 1966).

Presbyterians who had allied themselves in practice with the Fundamentalist Christians of the 1920s dedicated their lives as missionaries in Korea, so Korean Presbyterianism received a Fundamentalist imprint along with most of the other Korean Protestant Christian denominations. For the most part, all the Korean Protestant denominations consider Korean Roman Catholics as non-Christians, along the American Fundamentalist Christian lines in which they were educated. Even today, this position holds true for most Korean Protestants.

    Korean-American churches have followed the route of Korean Christianity and they tend to exhibit the characteristics of Conservative Presbyterianism combined with American Fundamentalist Christianity. This is true regardless of the denomination – whether Presbyterian, Methodist, Charismatic, Baptist, or Quaker. Thus, it is understandable why the Puritans play such an important role in Korean-American Christianity. Presbyterian-influenced Korean Christianity accentuates the Puritan origin of American history, not dissimilar to the aggressive push of American Presbyterian leaders, such as Rev. James D. Kennedy (PCA) and Rev. R. C. Sproul (PC USA). Thus, most Korean-Americans have no problem being loyal to Korea, "their country," and America, "the Christian country." For most Korean-American Christians, America represents a light unto the nations which has played a central role in the Christianization of the world.

    Of course, the Korean-American perception of the United States as a Christian nation is misguided. The United States is the only western nation in the world that legally forbids Christian prayer in its government funded schools. For instance, in Australia, tax money fund full-time Christian counsellors and Christian Bible study leaders to provide in-school and after-school Christian services to government-run high schools. In all the countries in Europe, Christianity is encouraged and often taught in the government funded school system. Many Southern Baptists in the USA have long described the USA as "the whore of Babylon" for what they perceive as American anti-Christian laws, including anti-

Christian legislation targeting the public school system. Many American Fundamentalist Christians refuse to vote and have even publicly praised the success of 9/11 attacks as a judgment of God on America. Both Rev. Jerry Fawell who represents a Baptist-type leadership and Rev. Pat Robertson who represents the Charismatic-type leadership – representing two Conservative Protestant Christian streams in the USA who are in conflict with each other historically – have described 9/11 as a judgment of God on America. Many American Christians privately share in this position although they may not publicly go on record to say that.

While American evangelical Christianity has developed along the lines of attacking the US government for its anti-Christian laws, Korean-American Christianity has not developed along with American evangelical Christianity because Korean-American churches tend to be self-contained within Korean-American communities. Korean-American churches, therefore, tend to ignore the American evangelical discourse and attack of US policies that generally exist within white American communities, associations, and churches. Korean-American Christian perception of America has been fixed in the 1960s or even before. And Korean-American churches have generally continued to paint a rosy picture of America as a Christian nation, actively sending out missionaries and Christianizing the world. Whereas most American evangelical Christians have a nuanced loyalty toward the United States, where they say they are patriotic to "America" but not to the US government which is anti-Christian, Korean-American Christians have, by in large, ignored such a discourse and simplified their relationship to the USA by calling America a Christian nation.

Of course, this reality is shifting radically, particularly among the American-born Korean-Americans who experience the anti-Christian government school system that conflicts with the kind of evangelical Christianity they experience at churches. But even in the case of American-born Korean-Americans, most Korean-American youth have tended to simplistically describe America as a Christian nation like their parents as Korean-American churches generally push that version of America. It is no surprise, therefore, that Korean-American communities tend to be quite patriotic to America, as immigrant communities go. More frequently than not, Koreans running for political office run on the Republican ticket.

For many Korean-American youth assuming that the United States was a Christian nation, 9/11 had a profound impact. Before 9/11, Korean-American youth did not think critically and aggressively about the question of America as a Christian nation. They just assumed that the United States was a Christian nation because that is what's generally taught in Korean-American churches. Korean-American youth often do not involve themselves in politics, so the opportunities for raising critically questions are limited on the political front. And most Korean-American Christians do not listen to or subscribe to American evangelical ministries – like white American Christians – so many of them are oblivious to the discourse among evangelical Christians regarding the anti-Christian nature of American laws and America's public institutions. Without 9/11, these Korean-American youths could have ignored this question and would have happily lived their life in a state of ignorance. However, 9/11 forced them to question realities that surround them.

When 9/11 hit America and the terrorist attack of bunch of Third World individuals infiltrated perhaps the most secure public domain of the US airport system, it showed Korean-Americans that God did not protect America. Whereas many white American Christians have long assumed that God did not protect America and in fact God wanted to punish America, Korean-Americans never really thought along those lines, before. 9/11 affirmed for many white American Christians the fact that God was alive and God delivered His judgement, so more white Americans went to a Christian church than before the 9/11 attack. The case was not the same for Korean-Americans. Many Korean-American youths started to leave the Christian church *en masse*. Many Korean-

American teenagers and college students became disillusioned with their Christian faith because Korean-American churches almost never explained the possibility of God punishing America, "the Christian nation," unlike many white Christian churches, which have for decades warned of impending judgement of God on America. Thus, from their Korean-American socio-cultural matrix, 9/11 represented a possibility that God did not exist and Christianity was false. Why would a Christian America be attacked successfully by a bunch of uneducated, unsophisticated, Third Word individuals? Obviously, Christian God was false and there was another true God or no God at all.

A strong stream of Korean-American Christians began to leave Korean-American churches after 9/11 and the trend is accelerating. For the Korean-American community, this is a serious and disturbing trend. Beside the implications for the Christian faith, Korean-American communities are becoming highly unstable. Unlike other immigrant communities, Korean-American churches are the primary ethnic centers for the Korean-American communities in the USA. High mobility away from Korean-American churches is creating a gap in Korean-American communal organization and cohesion. Many can easily become targets of Communist organizations and individuals, even those sponsored officially, albeit secretly, by North Korea for hostile purposes against the United States. This would not have been possible when most of the Korean-Americans were directly or indirectly associated with Korean-American churches, all of which are aggressively anti-Communist. Thus, it is not surprising to find that since 9/11, Korean-American youth have exhibited strong pro-China reference and stance and implicitly followed an anti-American direction. Such a phenomenon was non-existent or minimal before 9/11. Many Korean-Americans began to feel that "the Christian nation" can no longer defend them or their Mother Country. They, thus, began looking toward the competition for protection, support, and allegiance.

While one stream – perhaps the strongly greater trend – among the Korean-American youth has been toward divestment of allegiance to "the Christian nation" and configuring of loyalty to China, or an anti-American position (in large part directly tied to their leaving Korean-American churches and abandoning the Christian faith), there has been an opposite force pushing some Korean-Americans in the other direction. Those Korean-American youths who are not following the main trend, have gone the other way and have become more Fundamentalist Christian in their faith. Korean-American youth can be seen joining very conservative churches, such as Redeemer PCA in Manhattan, New York City, which represents a very conservative Presbyterianism. Many opt for such a conservative church over against churches where they grew up that tend to be less conservative. Even in seminaries, Korean-Americans can be seen as pushing a conservative trend. This is true of Princeton Theological Seminary of the Presbyterian Church (USA) as much as it is at Drew University, which trains for ordained ministry in the United Methodist Church (UMC). The Fundamentalizing trend of Korean-Americans who stay in the Christian faith do not seem to see any abatement at the moment. In fact, the process toward conservative evangelical Christian faith is accelerating in Korean-American churches across the 50 US states where Korean-Americans reside, regardless of denomination or particular Christian affiliation of these Korean-American churches. But this is not atypical. In fact, the majority of American churches are tending toward Fundamentalism at the moment, across all denominations. For instance, Presbyterian Church (USA) is being dominated by laity-led conservative movements that are now beginning to dictate the denominational direction. Similar trends are found in other mainline denominations, such as the Episcopalian Church and the United Methodist Church, where President George W. Bush has his membership.

Because 9/11 is still quite recent, it is difficult to determine the long-term impact on the Korean-American community. For now, we observe the two opposing trends among Korean-

American youth. The Korean-American youth divesting from Korean- American churches and tacitly renouncing loyalty to the United States is the stronger trend. Of course, as America is in the middle of The War on Terror, no one really knows what the future holds for the United States of America as a country. The majority of Americans believe that there will be a nuclear terrorist attack in the next five years. With South America becoming Communist and aligning themselves with Iran and China, Americans have more to fear than Bin Laden and Al Qaeda. A successful nuclear attack of Washington DC and New York City will destroy the United States of America as we know it and reshape the known world and history. The final chapter of the story begun by 9/11 is far from over. And Korean-Americans, being citizens of the United States, share the destiny of the United States, whichever trend they actively choose to follow.

Bibliography

Abelmann, Nancy, and John Lie. *Blue Dreams: Korean Americans and the Los Angeles Riots*. Cambridge: Harvard University Press, 1995.

Adams, Romanzo. *Interracial Marriage in Hawaii*. Montclair: Patterson Smith, 1937.

Alexander, Jeffrey C., and Steven Seidman (Editors). *Culture and Society: Contemporary Debates*. Cambridge: Cambridge University Press, 1990.

Baldassare, Mark (Editor). *The Los Angeles Riots: Lessons for the Urban Future*. Boulder: Westview Press, 1993.

Barringer, Herbert, Robert W. Gardner, and Michael J. Levin. *Asians and Pacific Islanders in the United States*. New York: Russell Sage Foundation, 1982.

Berger, P., and T. Luckman. *The Social Construction of Reality*. New York: Doubleday, 1966.

Bernal, M., and G. Knight (Editors). *Ethnic Identity: Formation and Transmission among Hispanics and Other Minorities*. Albany: SUNY Press, 1993.

Blalock, Hubert M. *Power and Conflict: Toward a General Theory*. Newbury Park: Sage Publications, 1989.

Blalock, Hubert M., Jr. *Toward a Theory of Minority Relations.* New York: Wiley, 1967.

Bonacich, Edna, and Lucie Cheng (Editors). Philadelphia: Temple University Press, 1994.

Che, Sunny. *Forever Alien: A Korean Memoir, 1930-1951.* Jefferson: McFarland & Company, Inc., Publishers, 2000.

Choi, Yong-Joon. *Dialogue and Antithesis: A Philosophical Study on the Significance of Herman Dooyeweerd's Transcendental Critique.* Cheltenham: The Hermit Kingdom Press, 2006.

Choy, Bong-Youn. *Koreans in America.* Chicago: Nelsen Hall, 1979.

Cohen, Nathan. *The Los Angeles Riots: A Sociological Study.* New York: Praeger, 1970.

Douglas, Jack D. *American Social Order.* New York: Free Press, 1971.

Edwards, Chon S. *I Am Also A Daughter of Korea.* Seoul: Mi-Rae-Mun-Wha-Sa, 1988. [in Korean]

Eriksen, Thomas. *Ethnicity and Nationalism.* London: Pluto Press, 1993.

Feagin, Joe R., and Clairece Booth Feagin. *Discrimination American Style.* Malabar: Robert E. Krieger Publishing, 1986.

Franklin, John H. (Editor). *Color and Race.* Boston: Beacon, 1969.

Gamson, William A. *The Strategy of Social Protest.* Belmont: Wadsworth, 1990.

George, Lynelle. *No Crystal Stair: African-Americans in the City of Angels.* London: Verso, 1992.

Goffman, Erving. *The Presentation of Self in Everyday Life.* New York: Doubleday, 1965.

Goldberg, David Theo. *Racist Culture: Philosophy and the Politics of Meaning.* Oxford: Blackwell, 1993.

Gooding-Williams, Robert (Editor). *Reading Rodney King/Reading Urban Uprising.* New York: Routledge, 1993.

Gordon, Milton M. *Assimilation in American Life: The Role of Race, Religion and National Origins.* New York: Oxford University Press, 1964.

Green, Charles. *The Struggle for Black Empowerment in New York City: Beyond the Politics of Pigmentation.* New York: Praeger, 1989.

Hing, Bill Ong. *Making and Remaking Asian America through Immigration Policy, 1850-1990.* Stanford: Stanford University Press, 1993.

Hodges, Harold M., Jr. *Conflict and Consensus: An Introduction to Sociology.* New York: Harper and Row, 1974.

Hunt, Bruce F. *For A Testimony.* Edinburgh: Banner of Truth, 1966.

Hurh, Won Moo. *The Korean Americans*. Westport: Greenwood Press, 1998.

Hurh, Won Moo, and Kwang Chung Kim. *Korean Immigrants in America: A Structural Analysis of Ethnic Confinement and Adhesive Adaptation*. Rutherford: Associated University Presses, 1984.

Kasinitz, Philip. *Caribbean New York: Black Immigrants and the Politics of Race*. Ithaca: Cornell University Press, 1992.

Kim, Byong-Suh, and Sang Hyun Lee (Editors). *The Korean Immigrant in America*. Montclair: The Association of Korean Christian Scholars in North America, Inc., 1980.

Kim, Hyung-Chan (Editor). *The Korean Diaspora: Historical and Sociological Studies of Korean Immigration and Assimilation in North America*. Santa Barbara: ABC-Clio, Inc., 1977.

Kim, Illsoo. *New Urban Immigrants: The Korean Community in New York*. Princeton: Princeton University Press, 1981.

Kim, Warren Y. *Koreans in America*. Seoul: Po Chin Chai Printing Co. Ltd., 1971.

Kinloch, Graham C. *The Dynamics of Race Relations: A Sociological Analysis*. New York: McGraw-Hill, 1974.

Kitano, Harry L. *Race Relations*. Englewood Cliffs: Prentice-Hall, 1974.

Kurokawa, Minako (Editor). *Minority Responses*. New York: Random House, 1970.

Kwak, Tae-Hwan, and Seong Hyong Lee (Editors). *The Korean-American Community: Present and Future.* Seoul: Kyungnam University Press, 1991.

Kwon, Ho-Youn (Editor). *Korean Americans: Conflict and Harmony.* Chicago: North Park College and Theological Seminary, 1994.

Kwon, Ho-Youn, and Shin Kim (Editors). *The Emerging Generation of Korean-Americans.* Seoul: Kyung Hee University Press, 1993.

Lee, Dae Kil (Editor). *The Current Status and Future Prospects of Overseas Koreans.* New York: Research Institute on World Affairs, 1986.

Lee, Shinyoung. *Impact of Ethnic Identity on Psychological Well-Being among Korean Americans in the United States.* Ph.D. dissertation for the School of Social Welfare, State University of New York at Albany, 2001.

Lewy, Thomas, and In Chul Choi. *The Korean American Entrepreneur's Guide to Franchising.* Chicago: Columbia College, Chicago, and Korean American Community Services, 1994.

Light, Ivan, and Edna Bonacich. *Immigrant Entrepreneurs: Koreans in Los Angeles, 1965-1982.* Berkeley: University of California Press, 1988.

Madhubuti, Haki R. (Editor). *Why L.A. Happened.* Chicago: Third World Press, 1993.

Mangiafico, Luciano. *Contemporary Asian Immigrants: Patterns of Filipino, Korean, and Chinese Settlement in the United States*. New York: Praeger, 1988.

Marger, Martin N. *Race and Ethnic Relations: American and Global Perspectives*. Belmont: Wadsworth, 1991.

Massey, Douglas, and Nancy A. Denten. *American Apartheid: Segregation and the Making of the Underclass*. Cambridge: Harvard University Press, 1993.

McCarthy, Cameron, and Warren Crichlow (Editors). *Race, Identity, and Representation in Education*. New York: Routledge, 1993.

Min, Pyong Gap. *Caught in the Middle*. Berkeley: University of California Press, 1996.

Min, Pyong Gap. *Ethnic Business Enterprise: Korean Small Business in Atlanta*. Staten Island: Center for Migration Studies, 1988.

Muhlmann, Wilhelm E. *Rassen, Ethnien, Kulturen: Moderne Ethnologie*. Berlin: Luchterhand, 1964.

Myrdal, Gunner. *An American Dilemma: The Negro Problem and Modern Democracy*. New York: Harper and Row, 1944.

Omi, Michael, and Howard Winant. *Racial Formation in the United States: From the 1960s to the 1980s*. New York: Routledge, 1986.

Park, Andrew Sung. *Racial Conflict and Healing: An Asian-American Theological Perspective*. Maryknoll: Orbis Books, 1996.

Park, Robert E. *Race and Culture*. Glencoe: Free Press, 1950.

Petersen, William. *Japanese Americans*. New York: Random House, 1971.

Roedinger, David R. *The Wages of Whiteness: Race and the Making of the American Working Class*. London: Verso, 1991.

Roosens, Eugeen E. *Creating Ethnicity: The Process of Ethnogenesis*. Newbury Park: Sage Publications, 1989.

Rosald, Renato. *Culture and Truth*. Boston: Beacon Press, 1993.

Rothschild, Joseph. *Ethnopolitics: A Conceptual Framework*. New York: Columbia University Press, 1981.

Schermerhorn, R. A. *Comparative Ethnic Relations: A Framework for Theory and Research*. New York: Random House, 1970.

Scott, A. J., and E. R. Brown (Editors). *South Central Los Angeles: Anatomy of an Urban Crisis*. Los Angeles: The Lewis Center for Regional Policy Studies, University of California, Los Angeles, 1993.

Shaw, Marvin E., and Jack M. Wright. *Scales for the Measurement of Attitudes*. New York: McGraw-Hill, 1967.

Shibutani, Tomatsu, and K. M. Kwan. *Ethnic Stratification*. New York: Macmillan, 1965.

Simpson, George E., and J. Milton Yinger. *Racial and Cultural Minorities*. New York: Harper, 1972.

Sleeper, Jim. *The Closest Strangers: Liberalism and the Politics of Race in New York*. New York: Norton, 1990.

Smith, Anna Deavere. *Twilight: Los Angeles, 1992*. New York: Anchor, 1994.

Sonenshein, Raphael J. *Politics in Black and White: Race and Power in Los Angeles*. Princeton: Princeton University Press, 1993.

Stone, John. *Racial Conflict in Contemporary Society*. Cambridge: Harvard University Press, 1985.

Terkel, Studs. *Race: How Blacks and Whites Think and Feel about the American Obsession*. New York: Anchor Books, 1993.

Totten, George O., III, and H. Eric Schockman (Editors). *Community in Crisis: The Korean Community after the Los Angeles Civil Unrest of April 1992*. Los Angeles: Center for Multiethnic and Transnational Studies, University of Southern California, 1994.

Turner, Victor. *The Ritual Process: Structure and Anti-Structure*. Chicago: Aldine, 1969.

West, Cornel. *Race Matters*. Boston: Beacon Press, 1993.

Wilson, William Julius. *The Truly Disadvantaged: The Inner City, the Underclass, and Public Policy*. Chicago: University of Chicago Press, 1987.

Wolf, Eric. *Europe and the People without History*. Berkeley: University of California Press, 1982.

Yu, Eui-Young (Editor). *Black-Korean Encounter: Toward Understanding and Alliance*. Los Angeles: Institute for Asian American and Pacific Asian Studies, California State University, 1994.

Yu, Eui-Young, Earl H. Phillips, and Eun Sik Yang. *Koreans in Los Angeles*. Los Angeles: Koryo Research Institute and Center for Korean-American and Korean Studies, California State University, 1977.

Yu, Eui-Young, and Edward Chang (Editors). *Multiethnic Coalition Building in Los Angeles*. Los Angeles: Institute for Asian American and Pacific American Studies, California State University, 1995.

Yuh, Ji-Yeon. *Beyond the Shadow of Camptown: Korean Military Brides in America*. New York: New York University Press, 2002.

Index

1st generation, 3, 4, 6
1.5 generation, 3, 5
2nd generation, 3, 5, 8, 17
3rd generation, 4, 5, 11
9/11, 1, 16, 18, 19, 20, 21, 22, 23, 24, 46, 184, 185, 193, 194, 195, 196
adhesive adaptation, 8
atheist, 93, 96, 104, 105, 111, 147
African-Americans, 28, 34, 36, 37, 52, 107, 111, 112, 114, 115, 116, 117, 118, 120, 177
African Methodist Episcopal, 52
Al Qaeda, 196
American Jewish Congress, 132
American Revolution, 50
anti-Communist, 13, 194
anti-white, 8, 12, 13, 189
Arabs, 124
Asia Center for Theological Studies, 54
Australia, 191
Austria, 6
Babylon, 191

Banana, 2, 3, 6, 8, 10, 11, 12, 82, 98, 134, 146, 150, 180
Bin Laden, 196
boycott, 113
British, 126
Brooklyn, 113, 114
Brown University Chapel, 56
Buddhist, 14, 15, 16, 20, 72, 81, 90, 147
Bush, George W., 61, 195
Calvinist, 53, 86
Cambridge, 52, 53
Cambridge Korean Theologians Association, 53
Campus Crusade for Christ, 55, 59
Caribbean, 127, 128
Chang, Won H., 88
China, 7, 24, 25, 73, 76
Chinese-Americans, 9, 29, 42, 93, 126, 129, 137, 138, 140, 141, 142, 143, 144, 147, 148, 149, 150, 179
Chink, 33, 36
Chong-Shin, 54, 58
Choy, Bong-Youn, 16
CIA, 24
Civil Rights, 34

Index

Civil War, 120
Claremont School of Theology, 53, 55
color, 34, 35, 36, 37, 38, 39, 40, 44, 86, 87, 92, 99, 100, 101, 102, 103, 104, 105, 119, 120, 121, 122, 130, 132, 178, 179
Communist, 13, 18, 150, 194
Confucian, 29, 30, 60, 70, 71, 72, 73, 74, 75, 76, 77, 79, 80, 81, 82, 83, 84, 85, 86, 87, 89, 90, 91, 163, 164, 165, 166, 167, 170, 172
Consulting, 99
Dallas Theological Seminary, 59
Democratic Party, 110, 122
Edwards, Chon S., 8
Edwards, Jonathan, 68
egg roll, 35
Eliade, Mercea, 72
engagement, 162, 163
Episcopalian Church, 195
Essenes, 72
evangelical, 1, 19, 22, 23, 46, 53, 55, 56, 58, 59, 60, 61, 62, 63, 64, 65, 66, 67, 68, 69, 147, 185, 192, 193
Fawell, Jerry, 59, 64, 192
FBI, 24
FOB, 2, 3, 6, 134, 175, 179
fraternity, 43
French, 126, 143

Fuller Theological Seminary, 49, 54, 59
Fundamentalist, 22, 23, 50, 53, 55, 56, 57, 58, 61, 63, 64, 91
German-Americans, 9
Germans, 126, 143
Graham, Billy, 59
Green Card, 151
Hagee, John, 60
Haifa, 125
Harlem, 113
Harvard, 41, 55, 58, 59, 60, 61, 81, 83, 97, 98, 91, 101, 102, 103, 130, 131
Hawaii, 10, 185, 186
Hellenistic, 71, 72, 73
Hermit Kingdom, 7
Hillel, 130
Hispanic, 38, 126, 127, 128, 137, 154, 171, 177
Holy Matrimony, 157, 162, 163
homosexuality, 54
Hoobae, 76, 77, 78, 79, 80
Hunt, Bruce, 190
Hurh, Won Moo, 5, 8, 10, 96, 99
hyung, 82
India, 157
InterVarsity Christian Fellowship, 55
Investment Banks, 99
Iran, 196
Irish, 6

Index

Israel, 124
Ivy League, 56, 59, 83, 132
Japanese, 13, 125, 126, 138, 140, 141, 142, 145, 164, 189, 190
Jerusalem Temple, 72
Jewish, 53, 71, 72, 73, 93, 96, 98, 102, 103, 104, 105, 111, 124, 125, 129, 130, 131, 132, 163
Joong-May, 161, 162, 165, 166, 167, 180, 181, 182
Katsura, Taro, 109
Kennedy, James D., 191
Kim, Kwang Chung, 8
Kim Samu, 15
Kim, Seyoon, 54
Kim, Yong Choon, 12, 50, 57
King, Rodney, 111
Kingdom of Christ, 24, 63, 64, 65
Koh, Harold, 139
Koh, Ton-He, 31
Korean-American church, 9, 10, 19, 20, 29, 32, 37, 39, 48, 49, 56, 57, 93, 95, 109, 112, 114, 137, 142, 153, 161, 167, 182, 183, 184, 187, 188, 189, 191, 192, 193, 194, 195, 196
Korean-American experience, 185
Korean Campus Crusade for Christ, 23
Korean Christian Fellowship, 23
Korean Methodist Seminary, 54
Korean War, 13, 150, 161, 167
Koreanness, 133, 135, 139, 147, 148, 174, 178, 179, 180
Ko-Shin, 56
Kwak, Tae-Hwan, 4
Lee, Sang Hyun, 19, 22
Lee, Seong Hyong, 4
Los Angeles Riots, 12, 111, 112, 114
MacArthur, John, 24, 60
Manhattan, 195
Masters Seminary, 60
Mexican-American, 28, 93, 113
Middle Ages, 156
MIT, 97
MTV, 167, 177
Nazareth, 125
New Jersey, 128
New Land, 170
North Korea, 1, 25, 26, 73, 75, 108, 150, 152, 185, 189, 194
Oral Law, 169
Orthodox Presbyterian Church, 190
Oxford, 53
Pai, Sunok Chun, 108
Pai, Young, 117

209

Index

Park, Billy, 56
Philippines, 109
Phillips Exeter Academy, 41
Philo of Alexandria, 71, 72
Post-modernism, 129
Presbyterian, 49, 50, 51, 109, 190, 191
Presbyterian Church USA, 52, 55, 195
Princeton Theological Seminary, 49, 55, 56, 190, 195
Princeton University, 68, 70
Puritan, 19, 176, 177, 190, 191
racist, 38
Rabbinic Judaism, 73
Reagan, Ronald, 61
Redeemer PCA, 195
Republican Party, 110
Rhee, Sang-O, 9, 27, 40
Rhee, Syngman, 183
Robertson, Pat, 59, 64, 192
Roman Catholic Church, 157
Roman Catholics, 50, 176, 177, 190, 191
ROTC, 24
sacrament, 162
Scandinavians, 132
Schwartzeneggar, Arnold, 6
Seoul National University, 84
sexual inhibition, 43
Shammai, 130
Shintoist, 147
Soh Kyongbo, 14
Son Center, 15

sorority, 43, 44
South Korea, 26, 70, 73, 74, 84, 108, 121, 179, 187, 189
Southern Baptist, 58, 59, 147, 191
Sproul, R. C., 191
Stanford, 42, 61, 83, 97, 98, 99
Student For Christ, 23
suburbia, 30, 170, 175
Sunbae System, 73, 76, 77, 78, 79, 80, 81
Swagger, Jimmy, 66
Taft, William Howard, 109
Third World, 177, 194
Tong-Hap, 51
Trinity Evangelical Divinity School, 59
UCLA, 23, 81, 83
Unification, 108, 109
United Kingdom, 53
United Methodist Church, 51, 52, 53, 56, 58, 195
United States, 7, 25, 26, 42, 45, 65, 70, 77, 81, 86, 87, 93, 108, 109, 110, 114, 116, 120, 125, 132, 134, 136, 138, 142, 144, 158, 167, 173, 174, 178, 186, 191, 193, 196
University of California at Berkeley, 23, 42, 86, 101
University of Chicago, 58, 60

Index

University of Pennsylvania, 41, 131
US census, 4, 186
US government, 4, 62, 121, 131, 186, 192
US Naval Academy, 24, 184
US passport, 17
Vietnamese-American, 35, 36, 42, 43, 44, 93
Wal-Mart, 171
West Point, 24, 184
Westminster Theological Seminary, 49, 58
World Zionist Organization, 132
Yale, 41, 55, 58, 59, 60, 99, 100, 130, 133, 140
Yi Dynasty, 70, 190
Yuh, Ji-Yeon, 8
Zen Lotus Societies, 15

About the Author

Heerak Christian Kim is Adjunct Professor of Biblical Studies at Asia Evangelical College and Seminary in Bangalore, India. He was the Raoul Wallenberg Scholar at the Hebrew University of Jerusalem in 1995-1996. And Professor Kim was the Lady Davis Fellow in the State of Israel from 1996-1997. Professor Kim was the President of the Cambridge University Korean Society and has also served as the Vice President of the Brown University Korean Graduate Students Association. Professor Kim was the Korean Language Interpreter of Palisades Park, New Jersey, Municipal Court from 2006-2007. Professor Heerak Christian Kim is ordained in the Korean Presbyterian Church in America (Ko-Shin) and has received the M.Div. degree from the denominational seminary in New Jersey – The Korea Theological Seminary in America. The Rev. Prof. Kim also studied at Fuller Theological Seminary (M.A. in Theology, 1996), Harvard Divinity School, Claremont School of Theology. The Rev. Prof. Kim has researched Jewish Studies at Harvard University's Department of Near Eastern Languages and Cultures, at Brown University, and at the Hebrew University of Jerusalem. The Rev. Prof. Kim has researched theology at Cambridge University in England and Heidelberg University in Germany. Professor Heerak Christian Kim is a leading expert of Hebrew, Jewish, and Early Christian studies and often delivers important academic papers around the world in global conferences.

Professor Heerak Christian Kim contributes weekly editorial articles for his column, "Education in America" in *Korean Phila Times*, a Korean-American newspaper for the Korean-American community.

www.ingramcontent.com/pod-product-compliance
Lightning Source LLC
Chambersburg PA
CBHW022058160426
43198CB00008B/273